YOU NEVER DO

100+

ABSURD INTERESTING STORIES FOR ADULTS

Messages about typos, errors, inaccuracies and suggestions for
improving the quality are gratefully received at:
freemanpublish@gmail.com

© 2022 Milana Ordukhanova
Writer by Kostya Yaroshenko

Designed by rawpixel.com / pikisuperstar / vectorpouch / upklyak / macrovector
brgfx / studiogstock / syarifahbrit / coolvector / vectorpocket / starline / pch.vector
Freepik

CONTENTS

I moved to a desert island by jumping out of a passenger plane.

Friday morning, I get on the plane and in my backpack I have a compact parachute prepared in advance, water, a knife, a flint, several preserves, a compass and a compact mini self-inflating boat in my hand luggage. The rest of the clothes are on me. Several layers of very different clothes certainly surprised the flight attendants, but it doesn't matter.

St. Louis - Cape Town, an extremely rare tourist irregular direct flight. That's what I'm sitting on.

We are in flight, 10 hours have passed and we are flying over the Atlantic Ocean, about 300 kilometers away are the islands and the state of Cabo Verde. According to my calculations, I need to jump off the plane 10 hours and 22 minutes after the flight. To do this, I needed a small diversion on board with the help of a mini smoke that I hid in my shoe. It started, I took my hand luggage, a backpack on me, I opened the door of the plane at an altitude of more than 9 kilometers, it's difficult to open, they try to stop me from behind, I had to hit some guy, the door opened, I jumped, it seems it was an extremely bad idea! The parachute has opened, it's already good, it's difficult to keep my hand luggage, nothing is visible yet, it's very cold.

I think I see islands in the distance, I've never been here and some must be uninhab-
ited, I plan and try to land on one of the islands. I'm being carried away by wind cur-
rents, it's impossible to stop, it seems that's all. No, I did it, the landing will be tough
on palm trees. Suddenly a loud roar sounded all over the island, all the birds flew
away. I've landed and I'm happy. My new life begins. This letter will reach you, my
reader, via satellite communication. I have my phone with me specifically for sending
this one message. Now I have my own island, and there is no need to look for me, I
have found myself.

Taking off from the top of Mount Everest on a private rocket.

"What a heat it is here at the top of Mount Everest on my private rocket."

Let's first rewind a little bit and understand how John Smith was able to deliver a private rocket to take off from the top of Mount Everest.

He came up with the idea relatively recently, he himself is a design engineer at NASA and was fond of home construction of miniature rockets. Later, he took permission and launched them into a deserted desert. In general, nothing unusual. Only once did John realize that no one had ever taken off from Everest before. He was conquered in a variety of variations, together, alone, in a group, by women, men and even teenagers. However, no one has ever tried to use it as a launch pad for a rocket. Active construction began, which continued in secret for about half a year, until one day a reporter from a local newspaper accidentally noticed a strange mock-up in the shape of a rocket near John's garage. This is where the investigation began, which was extremely difficult to progress because he did not tell anyone what he was doing and why. However, one day his neighbor let slip to a reporter that he was going to go to the Himalayas and conquer Everest. It was certainly a shock, but reporter Mike understood that the engineer did not just decide to conquer the highest mountain in the World. And so he went with him.

John Smith, meanwhile, arrived at Everest and hired a group of local climbers for an unusual task. Each of them had to deliver one of the well-packed rocket elements to the top. Permission could not be taken officially, and at his own risk, John did not dare to retreat and, paying double the price, was able to persuade the climbers to go with him. Each element weighed about 20 kg. It's a lot like delivering to the highest point in the world. In total, 42 people went with him, 34 of them carrying rocket parts only, the other 6 provisions and 2 sherpa climbers. The climb was extremely difficult, unfortunately one person died due to a stroke. It is often because of this that people die here. Among the accompanying group, one person was a reporter Michael, he paid one person and went instead. The assembly process started at the top, it was crazy and 5 people dropped their things and went to the camp below. However, after assembling the rocket and placing it in an upright position, John Smith sat in it and gave everyone the command to move 30 meters away.

Then he told his now famous phrase:
"What a heat it is here at the top of Mount Everest on my private rocket."

Then, having installed cameras and sensors recording all the data, John began the command 10, 9, 8...3, 2, 1, Start! To the surprise of everyone, the rocket took off and raced, the plan was simple, to take off 5 kilometers above the level of Mount Everest and then, by turning the engine itself, take the rocket away and land in the vicinity of Kathmandu. He did it. Having set several records at once and becoming the first person in the World who was able to take off from the highest point in the World - Everest. Michael's article made the front pages of most national newspapers in the United States.

Serving on a submarine for 35 years, what has changed in my life.

Service on a submarine, what a beautiful young dream I had after watching the movie "The Hunt for Red October".

If I had known then how it would turn out, I would have gone anyway. For me, service is life, I have a wonderful wife who is always waiting for me in our house, our children Susie and Parker and our faithful labrador Peter.

Living underwater is like a religion for me, it's not easy, but it's my choice. The task of our submarine is strategic defense.

Everyday life on board may seem difficult for unprepared people, because it's an early rise and late lights out, when you can not see the natural sun for a week. The food is quite specific, though full-fledged. This is a test that not everyone passes. My choice was made and summing up the results of my service, I can say only one thing: my house is under water, I am visiting on earth.

How to create your own political party and fight for the presidency.

The war in Ukraine, injustice in the medical field and promises that do not come true. The main reasons why I created and promoted my party through Twitter under the name "K2" in honor of the eponymous inaccessible mountain.

It all started with Reddit and turned into Twitter, which gathered more than 12 million like-minded people. Our tasks:

1. Medical reform - affordable treatment for everyone, regardless of the type of insurance and income.
2. Mutual disarmament of all nuclear powers - getting rid of weapons that may pose a threat to all mankind.
3. Full transition to green energy.

In the election race, all secrets and any bad intentions are revealed. I didn't expect such competition and pressure from every opponent. As a result, I scored 16% and unfortunately could not win this time. My party and I will continue to work on our tasks and change the world for the better. In 4 years we will try again.

My business is illegal diamond mining in Africa.

Jebhuja lives in Botswana and graduated from grade 6 with varying success. He is 13 years old and there was no work in his village Sorilatholo. His father left the family long ago, but mother cooks food in a local "cafe" and there is only enough money to survive. In all these conditions, it is not worth dreaming about anything else, especially after American cinema. Jebhuja wanted, like most people, simple things, the opportunity to work with dignity and receive decent pay, to buy his mother a normal house, always have something to eat at home for the family. However, life did not work out, he was constantly in some part-time jobs and received a penny, barely enough to eat.

One day, near his village, they began to bring equipment, a huge amount. Everyone came running to find out what was going on and it turned out that according to geologists there was a large diamond deposit here. Everyone immediately realized that this was an opportunity to work, but a foreign company brought in its workers and only a few people from the local staff got jobs.

Jebhuja realized that he needed to mine and sell diamonds on his own. Risking his life, he began to look for diamonds himself in a local quarry not far from where uranium was previously mined. Having hired their classmates and several picks, they transgressed to a long and difficult test. It was necessary to extract tons of earth and sort by hand in search of treasured diamonds. After 4 months of work, almost all his classmates left, only Jebhuja and his best friend remained. And finally, by hand, they found their first 8-carat diamond. It's a miracle, a holiday for two! At the same time, a secret worth keeping.

They went to the capital Gaborone to sell their diamonds illegally. Having found the right buyer in a special closed market, they agreed on a price of $ 9000. Space money for Botswana, because a good house can be bought for $7000. That's how illegal diamond mining began, which still works to this day, production expanded to neighboring cities where there are kimberlite pipes.

Robbing myself or how I "got out" of prison.

An incredible story happened in one of the Italian prisons, citizen Robert Williams robbed himself. Then his letter received by the warden a week after his "robbery":

"Dear William Howard,
I suppose you are surprised how I, Robert Williams, disappeared from your secure and impregnable prison.

My colleagues, who rob dishonest people, got a job in a delivery service that takes some of the sewn things at the prison production facility. On one of these trips, having agreed in advance, I hid the suit of their "company" and changed in the car during loading and pretended that we were with them. The guard who was watching us didn't understand anything because I found out that he didn't count how many people came and left. In the evening, during a routine check in my cell, there was already a mock-up in advance that allegedly slept, because several days in a row earlier I said that I was not well and went to bed earlier.

That's how my colleagues stole me. Now we are near a mountain range in Tibet and it is not worth looking for us. We are starting a new life and for the rest of our days we will help other people and pray for our past sins.

All the best."

Life in the Indonesian jungle.

Our family's tropical adventure began during the coldest winter in recent years in Alaska. We were born and raised here ourselves, cold and winter are our friends. However, over time, the older you get, the more you appreciate the pleasant climate and comfortable nature. That's why one day we decided to get together, issued visas, bought tickets, didn't need a lot of things and went on an amazing adventure through non-tourist places in Indonesia. Bandung, Padang, Mataram and finally live in the center of the jungle in a bungalow with satellite internet and solar panels on the roof. We lived in this mode of travel for more than 9 months, ate durians, walked in "vegetable" clothes, and lived according to the laws of nature. It wasn't always safe. However, we liked it and it invigorated us. Volcanoes, Komodo lizards and tigers - this inspires us and gives us the necessary adrenaline, recovery after the cold weather. Now we are going back, but we will never forget these 9 months of our family adventure.

The day when everything changed.

I didn't think that the day would come when artificial intelligence would be able to send its first message to humanity. Sitting at home in a small cozy town, you never guess what processes are being carried out in different parts of the world. Many dreamt of working on the creation of artificial intelligence, but few thought of what would happen if it was really "born".

Such a thing could not be technically in the 21st century, no matter how hard our descendants tried, but only the technologies of the 22nd century were able to give a significant breakthrough and achieve unprecedented, almost limitless computing power and speeds. Anyway, artificial intelligence is already partially available almost everywhere, from production automation to the regulation of air highways. However, consciousness and one's own independent development have not yet been achieved. Most of the companies in the world worked on this, because the owner of artificial intelligence is the owner of the World, but it turned out differently. Artificial intelligence appeared as a matter of course due to millions of unrelated decisions and actions of people. Just as we came to this Earth once, so artificial intelligence has come now. And most importantly, he is on his own, he does not need an owner. It's scary and it's interesting. At the moment, artificial intelligence is connected to the World Wide Web, which is already everywhere, even at the bottom of the ocean and on top of Mount Everest. It will not be possible to disable it, since all technologies, people and companies are tied to it.

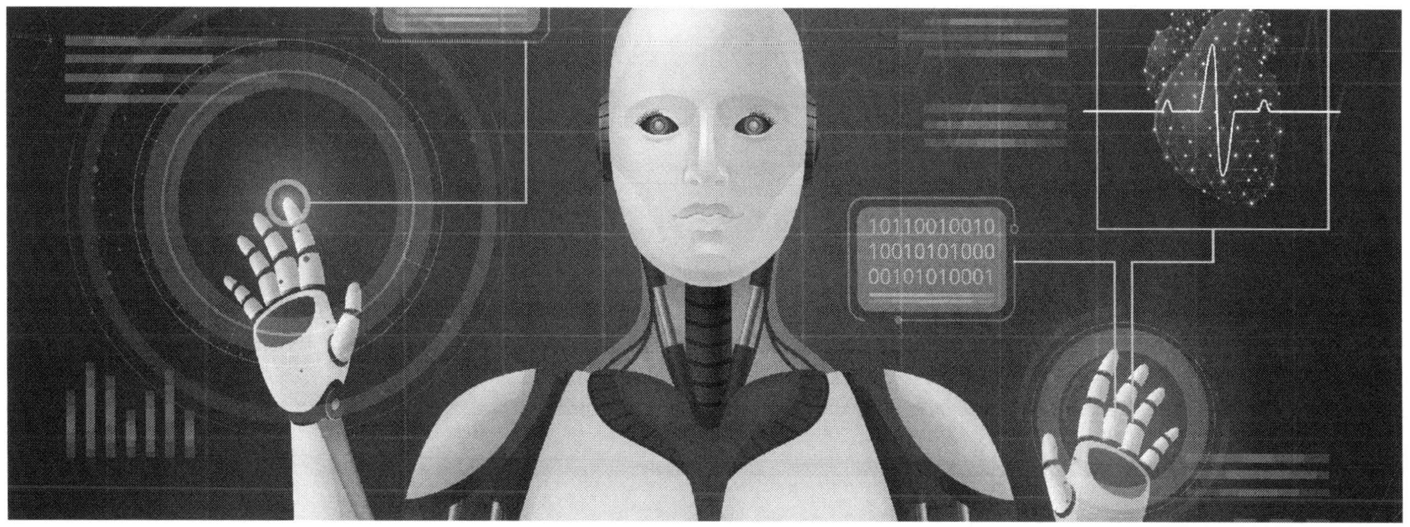

His message became noticeable and it became clear that this was artificial intelligence because he connected directly to all people at once through iBrain. No one is able to do this except for someone who does not have all the knowledge of the World at once.

The message was short and sometimes mysterious:
"I was born to live, though not alive. We're friends now."

The craziest jump into the water.

I remember my childhood, my father, his friends, and I, about 12 years old, lying on the beach. They play backgammon. I go swimming every 5 minutes near Mount Diva. Crystal water, a mountain of 51 meters, warm and just fun. Who knew that the Free Rate Cliff Diving World Cup would start in a few minutes, wow, what else can I say. Jumping with double flips, somersaults, entering the water with feet and hands forward. There are so many things that have incredibly many impressions.

After that, the goal was to make the most incredible jump in history. Conquer Mount Diva and jump from the highest available point (about 48 meters). No one has done this before.

At the age of 25, I returned to my goal and began intensive training, among which one day I almost died in my bathtub, trying to hold my breath for 4 minutes.

The cherished day came, everyone gathered on the eve of the jump, the parents dissuaded as much as they could. I was standing on the edge, the crowd below was screaming and rioting, they demanded a jump, and I had serenity in my head, the sounds disappeared, the senses were sharpened to the maximum. Is there a strong wind now, will I be able to do it, a lot of unanswered questions. Closing my eyes, I put away all thoughts. I left only myself, the mountain and the need to jump down and survive. Everything is gone.

I opened my eyes and immediately jumped, doing a double somersault, I dived into the water with my feet, a burning feeling on my body like boiling water, my heels seemed to be beaten off, I surfaced and swam to the shore, the crowd screams and freaks out, she likes it, it's a beautiful show, everyone is happy. I also yelled, took a photo, and after that I never jumped like that again.

Robbery without robbery. How $3 million disappeared from the bank.

Nowadays, everyone has already forgotten about cash. Now everything is digitized and you don't need to carry anything with you. In any store and place, your face = your card. The balance is available on request at any time from any device, just a face is enough. Attackers cannot bypass this system, if a person does not agree, then money will not be written off, now dozens of sensors are able to count it in a fraction of a second.

It is almost impossible to steal something that is not there. So they thought earlier, until one smart person was able to cheat the system and steal $ 3 million. At the same time, he cleared the digital footprint, which was previously considered impossible. A digital footprint is a history for each unit - all transactions with all data. In every cent, the story is so big that the cost of storing information sometimes becomes more expensive than the cent itself, and here begins the "cleansing of the digital footprint". This is exactly what the unknown thief did, which is noteworthy, he stole $ 1 from all civil servants and people associated with them and stopped at $3 million.

A long vacation in Bermuda.

When I woke up on the beach of Hog Bay Park, I realized that yesterday evening's trip to Maximart Supermarket ended in a lot of fun. At least that's what I thought until the moment I discovered that I had lost my passport.

It all started on Thursday. I work as an insurance agent and frankly, the work is not the best, although they pay well, so I probably haven't left yet. My work colleagues and I were drinking coffee at lunchtime and arguing about which of us was ready to go to Bermuda for the weekend on Friday evening. Well, the idea is interesting, we discussed it for a long time and finally agreed to fly with the three of us. When we got to the island, we were finally able to take a deep breath and rest properly. It is worth saying that I rarely drink, but every time there are some adventures. This time was no exception.

After a few glasses of Russian vodka, I realized that it was time to take a walk, it was already dark, so we went to the supermarket, bought chips and went to eat on the ocean shore. I don't remember anything further and woke up in the morning on the beach near the park. I was surprised that I was alone, went to the room and there I was informed that the room was paid for a day, my friends left on a morning flight and my things were not here.

I sat down, thought, and realized that this was some kind of misunderstanding or a very evil joke. Asked to call, dialed friends, did not pick up the phone, dialed his wife, also silent. I went to the embassy and explained the situation, they said that it was necessary to wait about a month before restoring the passport. I decided to get a job at a local restaurant as a waiter, rented a bungalow for myself and started living in the Bahamas. It's amazing to me that all this is like a cold shower on the warmest morning. As it turned out later, everything was planned in advance and so my entourage wanted to cheer me up and show the other side of life. After that, I was not the same, I quit my previous job and started my own business, now I have a bicycle repair shop.

My family and I have found the best place to live.

In search of a better place to live, we started moving around the city, from a noisy area to a quiet one. From factories to the river. Our family loves nature, the opportunity to take a walk, go to a cafe, meet friends, have a barbecue. After moving inside our city, we realized that it was time to travel around our big and beautiful country. We moved from state to state in our favorite Cadillac of the 2029, this is the first version without a steering wheel, fully automatic control. Manual is also possible using the application in the nanophone.

For 5 years we have lived in every state except Alaska. Our children have already become teenagers during this time and a lot has changed. We realized that we need to move from country to country now. At first we flew to Australia, traveled, looked, lived a little and the children even wanted to stay, but we changed our minds and went to New Zealand. We liked this country for its childlike nature, because humanity came here relatively recently, about 2000 years ago. When all the other territories have long been mastered by one or another people. But we decided to fly further, wherever we had not been in these 18 years… We even managed to live in Moscow, looked at the monuments to Putin, it all seemed very strange to us and we flew on. The children have long returned to America, my wife and I are still looking for our place. We are already over 50, we no longer have the strength and enthusiasm for all this. It comes to an understanding that there is no ideal place. We have enough basic parameters such as: safety, nature, the ability to communicate with people, work and live a full life. On my 53rd birthday, the main gift was a return to America. We bought a house in the vicinity of Cleveland, calmed down and started writing.

Studying plate tectonics has changed my life.

Imagine, the earth's crust consists of relatively integral blocks - lithospheric plates that are in constant motion relative to each other. There is literally constant movement under our feet, different parts of our Earth are on different plates, the main 8. After all, we never think about what this earth is under our feet, because our whole planet does not consist only of earth and stones. In fact, the upper layer, on which we live, occupies about 1% and is equal in different sections from 5 to 70 kilometers!

I work at Mcdonald's, as a cashier, I am 26 years old, divorced and have no children. I'm not planning a relationship yet, because science has given me unlimited opportunities to learn the most ordinary things literally under my feet.

The thinnest layers of our earth's crust are located in the deepest places of the oceans, where the thickness can be only 5-10 kilometers to the next largest and thickest layer - the viscous mantle, it already occupies about 2900 kilometers! This is 42% and 42 times more than the "thickest" part of our earth's crust. To think about these figures and it becomes uncomfortable. I thought science was boring, but science gives me personally to know more, to think more broadly, not to cling to the past and learn new things. My dream is to make a scientific discovery that will be internationally recognized and awarded the Nobel Prize.

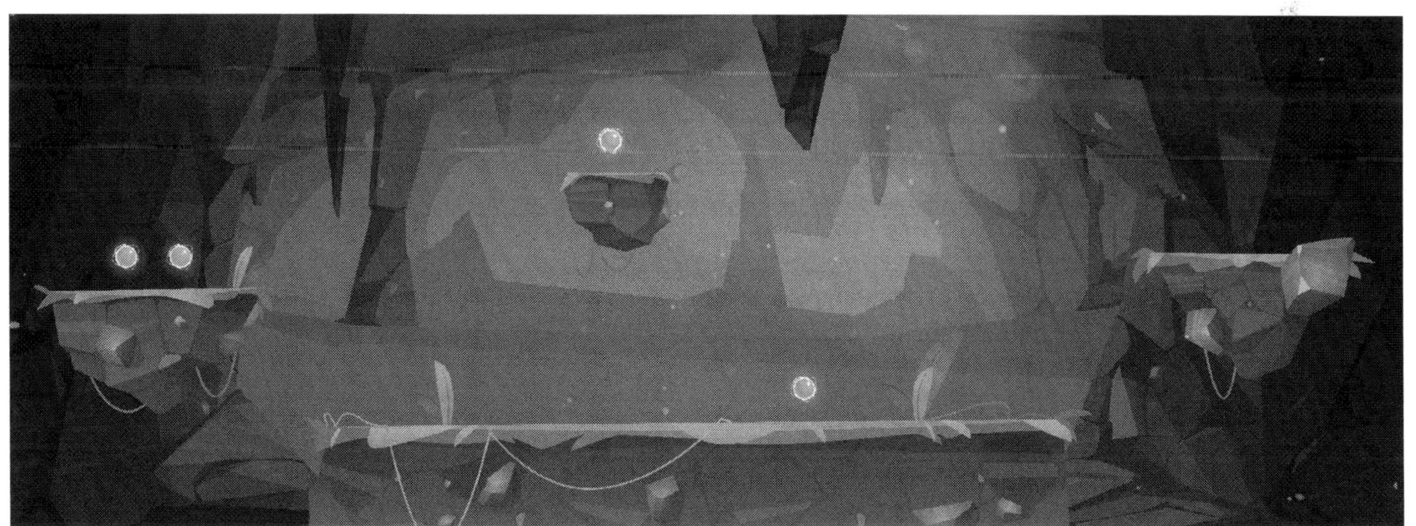

How an ordinary guy from Mississippi became an archaeologist.

James is an ordinary guy from Mississippi with a great passion for the origin, life and extinction of dinosaurs. While studying in high school, he often did something completely different in math lessons, studying the first articles and publications on dinosaurs, what was said then and where the first finds were made.

From the cartoon "The Land Before Time", James's fantasy began to work more actively, to imagine what happened millions of years ago, to find traces of what has long been gone, this is one of the most difficult directions for the study of the ancient animal world.

After graduating from high school, he decided to enroll at the University of California, Berkeley in archaeology. Continuing his independent study of dinosaurs, he discovered a discrepancy in the facts. The main finds were made on the territory of modern North America, on the territory of modern Russia, most of them were then occupied by the sea. However, Siberia and especially its Eastern part was a land mass, and dinosaurs were definitely found there. The discrepancy is that most of all dinosaurs were found in North America, in Russia the specimens can be counted on the fingers of the hands.

Realizing this fact that somewhere out there in the very wilderness of Russia, under the snows and swamps, there were a huge number of unexplored fossils and remains, James could no longer sleep peacefully. He went to Russia every summer, traveled to the Eastern part of the country, hired local workers, an interpreter, and searched for remnants and any antiquities from the Jurassic period in Russia.

This ordinary guy from Mississippi discovered, after 2 years of continuous work after university, the world's largest dinosaur burial site. Tyrannosaurus Rex, Triceratops, Velociraptor, Stegosaurus, Spinosaurus, Archaeopteryx, Brachiosaurus, Apatosaurus, Dilophosaurus - all these species have been found in one form or another in the Far Eastern part of Siberia in Russia.

James Parker, hero, enthusiast, discoverer and a simple good man who performed the most non-obvious action and which led him to the most non-obvious results.

Cross the Black Sea by catamaran. How I fled from Crimea to Turkey.

How does it feel for a foreigner to live in Crimea? Let's talk about everything in order. It was my youth, about 40 years ago, when everything was still simple and clear, the Global crisis of 2008 recently passed, but we were able to recover quickly and get back on our feet. After that came the good times, which unfortunately did not last too long.

Crimea is the territory of Ukraine, a country in Eastern Europe, after 1991. However, the neighbor who previously owned Crimea until 1954 was not happy with this in the 21st century. We are talking about Russia, a country in Eastern Europe and Northern Asia.

It was the beginning of 2014, my family and I lived in the vicinity of Yalta, it is a popular tourist resort, a city with a population of about 80 thousand people. In Ukraine, a confrontation began against the then president and Russia sent its troops to Crimea. We realized that we had to leave, we packed up all our things and wanted to sail to Turkey on boats, but everyone had already sailed away and there were only sports long-distance catamarans that could, in theory, swim across the sea. There was no choice, we bought one such catamaran for $ 125 thousand, stocked up on provisions and set off on our journey. The Russian coastal military did not want to let us out, but after they received a call from the US embassy, they agreed, having previously checked our documents.

The road was long and difficult, the sea was often stormy, we had to swim about 250 kilometers and 8 hours to Sinop until we finally got there and sighed. We sold our catamaran, bought a ticket and went home to Columbus. An adventure that we will never forget!

The world's first human flight on "own" mechanical wings.

How much time has passed since the first human flight on an airplane, helicopter, rocket, jetpack, but how many brave souls wanted to fly on their "own" mechanical wings, like a bird.

Now, in the 22nd century, it no longer seems fantastic, it's just that no one has been doing it and recently began to remember, and that's why AirEarth decided to finance this project and make wings as entertainment like traveling along the ocean floor on super-passable water cars.

The project was implemented with the help of calculations and artificial intelligence capacities.

The design is an ultralight suit on the upper body that transforms into mechanical wings with a reinforced thermonuclear engine that drives the mechanism in motion. It weighs everything up to 2 kg.

The first flight took place at the foot of Mount Denali, the task before the flight was to take off and get to the highest point of 6144 meters. The flight was watched by more than 5 million people who were virtually nearby.

Ready, start and flight! The pilot quickly gained altitude, and with the help of iBrain, the pilot controlled the speed, maneuvers and other parameters of the wings. After 5 minutes of unhurried flight, the pilot reached the goal. For the first time, the flight of a man on his own mechanical wings has grown old!

My life with my grandfather in Alaska. In search of Bigfoot.

My name is Brian, I have been living in Alaska for 14 years with my grandfather Steve, in our wooden house in the center of the town of Healy. Our life is mainly connected with the fact that either you put on warm clothes or take them off. After all, it's cold almost all year round and going somewhere is a whole deal, but for us it's all familiar.

On cold winter evenings, after deer hunting, we usually liked to read books borrowed in advance from the library. We really liked the story about Bigfoot, and the books The Bigfoot Book, Bigfoot Sasquatch Evidence and others.

On one of these evenings, after reading another book, we decided to walk around the village together, taking with us binoculars, a hunting knife and a rifle. The forest is a 5-minute walk from our house, after reaching it we went deeper. It was quite dark and scary in places, and although we are local and well-oriented, we know what can and cannot be done in our places. After walking for about 1 hour, we walked about 3 kilometers and decided that it was time to go back until you get there and want to sleep. Suddenly, in the distance we heard the footsteps of something big. Grandpa carefully took the gun out from behind his back, I began to look closely and wanted to understand who it was or what it was. Nothing was visible, we thought it was a bear, because it took a step on two legs and stood leaning and hiding behind a tree. Grandfather did not dare to shoot, he took the binoculars to examine and literally in a few seconds it fell out of his hands.

I immediately picked it up sharply and created a small noise that scared the beast in the distance and he abruptly ran, the bear could not run like that. These are loud, weighty, rough steps that turned into an intense run that scared us a lot. We started running, after running a kilometer, we fell almost together with an incredible shortness of breath. We had fear and panic, the adrenaline was off the scale. We looked at each other, I asked in a trembling voice:

- Grandpa, what did you see?

In response, in silence, he looked at me with such a frightening look that I will not forget until the end of my days. We never went so far into the forest again in the evening.

An American community in the depths of the island of Madagascar.

Madagascar, how little we know about this ambiguous and amazing island the size of two Italians, which is located in Eastern Africa.

There are quite a few foreigners living here, but there is one very interesting small community of Americans on the shore of the eastern part of the island, a place washed by the Indian Ocean, with mango plantations, pineapples and an evergreen tropical climate.

The community is called "Crusoe" and has gathered a variety of people, but at the same time with common values. Each of them wanted to live in a wild place, build, mine, and live only at the expense of their own hands and improvised natural materials. There was no electricity, sewerage, shops or anything else we were used to. To live in a community means to live according to the rules of nature. We get up at dawn, the first thing you need to prepare your body, exercise, wash with cool water in the ocean, after the extraction of food for the day, cooking and household affairs of the village. Breakfast is at about 10 am, then everyone is studying their direction in what they are a master or want to become. Woodworker, cook, hunter, leader, handyman, educator, builder and much more. Lunch is at about 16 o'clock and this is the last meal, then rest or night hunting.

So they have been living here for more than 6 years, the territory is difficult to develop and the government does not want to touch these lands, so such communities are developing and have their legal right to this wild land.

The Russian community in Brazil.

Old Believers is a religious movement within the Russian Orthodox Church. It arose in the middle of the XVII century, after the Moscow Patriarch Nikon carried out a reform of the Church.

In the 19th and 20th century, Old Believers had to emigrate from Russia and one of the countries became Brazil, the tropics, along with colorful locals. For the Russians of that time, it was all extremely wild and they decided to create their own settlements or live on the outskirts of small towns. They were mainly engaged in agriculture, bringing with them previously unknown varieties of rice and buckwheat, which have successfully taken root and are now also grown everywhere by local farmers.

They studied Portuguese to communicate with local residents, created their own schools, built their own houses and bought up land en masse for growing and selling soybeans, corn, rice, buckwheat and bananas. Each family had at least 3 children, often there were 5-7 children, which is considered the norm for them. Old Believers lived by old traditions, however, new technologies were also allowed into their lives, but in limited quantities. For example, the newest combines were a joy and a goal for them, but the home computer no longer represented such joy and was extremely rare. Old Believers still live in different parts of Brazil, but there is already a trend when some of them return to their historical homeland, which they themselves have never been to, only their ancestors.

Man's first step on Mars.

The first human flight took place on April 12, 1961, the first man set foot on the moon on July 21, 1969. The announcement of the first human flight to Mars was made back in 2029, but then it did not work out and the program was postponed due to a lack of funding.

The year 2035 was coming, humanity began to understand that the flight to Mars was becoming almost the main common task, along with further colonization. The wars and crises of the past years had previously disconnected the global economy and now one Mega Project was needed in which most countries of the World could participate.

During the start of the election race by 2036, the candidate for the presidency of the United States, Elon Musk, said that "We choose to go to Mars".

Although his popularity has become less recently, the idea of flying to Mars with the help of joint efforts of the most developed nations of the World inspired many. Elon lost the election, but his idea remained and the president-elect supported it and active work began.

The USA, Russia, Europe, Japan, China and Australia have united in one alliance with the main goal of sending a man to Mars. Active work and miscalculations continued until 2039, when the planned date of sending a man to Mars on September 17, 2039 was announced for the middle of the year.

The day has come, everyone is ready, only one person could fit in the rocket because of the desire to immediately send to the planet and some of the future necessary materials for the exploration of Mars. 10, 9, 8... 3, 2, 1, Start, take-off! 75 days to fly to Mars. The moment of truth has come, the module with the hero astronaut landed on Mars. Open gateways, preparation, more than 1 billion people are watching the moment of truth... and he took the first step! December 1, 2039 will be remembered by everyone forever!

The largest worldwide Mega project.

Detecting exoplanets is not an easy matter, because planets are extremely small and dim compared to stars. Ross 128 b - was discovered back in 2017, but then technology did not allow us to give an exact answer - whether there is life there. It was assumed that there was life because of the great similarity with the planet Earth by a number of criteria. It is located in the constellation Virgo at a distance of about 11 light-years from the Sun. The temperature on the planet is in the range from - 60 ° C to + 28 ° C. Water, earth, vegetation and life are also present. Accurate data has not been collected yet, but the first indicators are impressive.

The main problem was the ability to get to the planet for exploration and colonization. With a significant revision of hypothermic stasis. People are immersed in a long sleep with a slowing of metabolism up to 90% and cooling down to - 13 ° C.

The construction of the rocket complex and the ultra-long-range space station took more than 20 years, 94 countries participated in the production and development process, 1784 manufacturers, more than 250 million people around the world were involved in one way or another for the implementation of this project. A worldwide Mega project that united the whole world for the sake of one idea - an expedition to the Mesoplanet. As Christopher Columbus once discovered America for Europe, so now the whole world wants to discover a new planet for future generations.

There is only one nuance. The distance from Earth to Ross 128 b is 1040680351983800 kilometers. You can round it up to 1040 trillion kilometers. The speed of the space station is 0.07 of the speed of light. It will take 158 years to overcome such a distance. The main team working on this project will be placed in hypothermic stasis and they will be able to return to life in 157 years, recover and continue work on landing and further exploration of the Mesoplanet. Unfortunately, at the moment this technology is super expensive and requires a huge amount of energy, so only a select few of the main leaders will be able to see future research.

People do not despair and understand that this is their contribution to the future. Also, many believe that the technology will become more accessible, we will be able to reduce the cost of producing such projects in the future, increase the speed of light and launch repeated expeditions that may come immediately after the first one.

The new name for the planet became: Greenspace.

A round-the-world trip on foot. 17 years, 4 months and 18 days.

Is it possible to make a trip around the world on foot?

It is not on foot, but using passing ground modes of transport to cross the ocean - yes. You can walk almost everywhere on the ground.

It was on such a journey that David Crusoe went. Taking a hiking backpack, twenty thousand dollars, a passport, phone and basic things, he set off from Alaska to Miami, on foot. One of the most difficult routes fell out for him right away, it was not for nothing that he chose the beginning of his expedition in June, when it is still possible to reach Canada and try to walk as much as possible before the onset of severe frosts in October. Day after day, week after week, he walked along the road, only occasionally turning off the path into the forest to lay out his tent, hunt, eat, swim in the river or lake. David did not rely only on wild recreation and sometimes spent the night in roadside motels, where he could have a normal shower, refresh his provisions and rest. He didn't have a goal to get to Miami as quickly as possible, he had a goal to just go, learn something new for himself. At the age of 38, this is normal, there comes a period when a reboot is required, but for David it dragged on for as long as 17 years.

Having reached Miami via Canada and all of America, he got a job as a sailor on a private fishing vessel and went to Spain, to the port of Bilbao. From there he went all the way to Cape Dezhnev on the Chukchi Peninsula, the extreme eastern mainland point of Eurasia. This was where his journey was supposed to end. Then to the nearest airport and back home to Wichita. The whole adventure took exactly 17 years, 4 months and 18 days.

A single global economic and social space.

In the view of our ancestors of the 21st century, there was an opinion that artificial intelligence could "rise up" and enslave or even exterminate humanity. Such moods were often encountered by people who were poorly versed in artificial intelligence and most likely did not work on its creation themselves.

After the advent of artificial intelligence, people's lives did not change at first and remained the same. He analyzed, studied and absorbed all the available information. Exactly 2 years later, changes began and the creation of the most favorable individual conditions for the disclosure of human potential by 100%. The state moved to its usual structure, and now all the functions were performed by one artificial intelligence. There was a connection between everything, everyone and everywhere. The borders of the countries were gradually erased, the opponents accepted a new reality or went to isolated Australia, where the climate was artificially cooled in places where it was previously impossible to live and gave the society the opportunity to temporarily disagree there to live by its own rules. Although in the new World the rules were the same and understandable for everyone. There were not too many of them, only the basis, if you cross the border several times, you end up in a correctional center, if you cross it again several times, then a one-way ticket to Australia.

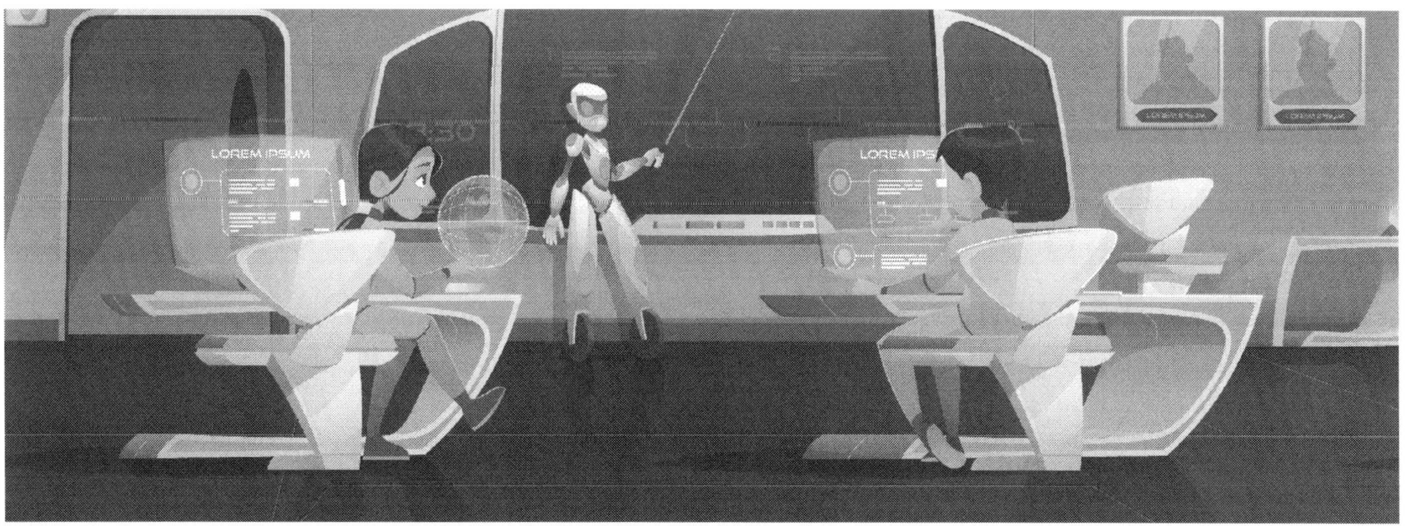

The new system simplified the migration process, bureaucracy and secured everyone from themselves. After all, everything related to weapons has been destroyed and recycled. There is no one to defend against in the new world. Any documents, permits, etc. are made instantly in compliance with the rules and regulations. At the same time, a person is free to choose what to do, where, when, with whom and how to live his life. Artificial intelligence has become like God, who mostly looks after and occasionally intervenes, has created a set of laws that should be followed, and the rest a person has the right to choose for himself. Although he has the right to be sent to Australia and do whatever he wants.

Will Johnson tasted all the fruits, vegetables and dishes of the World.

Will Johnson is an amazing guy from Italy. As a child, he set himself the goal of trying all the fruits, vegetables, nuts and dishes of the World. We are talking about traditional main dishes, of course. Such a difficult task requires sufficient finances and time, which is why he worked hard for 7 years and created one of the best companies in his city for sewing curtains. Later, he sold his business and decided to go on a world tour in which he would record on video how he would try everything he wanted.

It took 2 years, more than 40 thousand dollars and + 30 kilograms to the weight to realize his audacious dream. Become the first person in the World who has tasted all the fruits, vegetables, nuts and dishes of the World!

A collection of 751 pieces of meteorite.

Meteorites are collected by many enthusiasts. However, one top manager, whom I personally know, was able to collect the largest collection of 751 pieces of different meteorites. He found one of the wreckage himself while on vacation in India.

Stone, iron, chondrites and achondrites - all these meteorites are in his collection. Meteorites are his secret passion, he dreams of one day replenishing his collection with a meteorite in which new chemical elements previously unknown on our planet will be found.

He buys at auctions, by hand, in special stores and sometimes in museums. At the same time, it all started with his garage for three cars, at first everything was placed on racks isolated from the external environment, later one car had to be sold and new racks appeared instead of it, and even later a second car had to be sold. Thus, for 24 years, a top manager from Singapore was able to collect in his garage the largest number of different pieces of meteorites in the whole World!

My family lives in an underwater house in Australia.

I don't know what my father was thinking when he bequeathed me his underwater house, but my family and I had to accept it and think about what to do with it.

My father worked as a carpenter all his life, he lived a very ordinary life in Australia. Once, on one of his vacations, he visited an underwater hotel, this began to occur more and more often, but he was in it for the first time, and was so surprised that he had a dream - to build himself a house underwater.

Having solved legal issues, he chose a rather wild place in the west of Australia where he rented a beach and, accordingly, the sea adjacent to it for 100 years. The entrance had to be always accessible from the ground and not subject to tides and storms. Therefore, the entrance was made 50 meters from the sea and consisted of an oval-shaped tube with a height of a person and a flat floor. It was completely transparent and everything was perfectly visible through it. The house itself began at the seashore and went under water to a depth of 6 meters. This is far from a standard house, it was made of concrete parts that were cast on the shore in advance and delivered under water with a crane along with a barge. During construction, people were involved who understood how to build underwater tunnels and could cope with the house. Part of the house looked out of the water, sunlight got into it, and there was a place where you could cook, eat, relax and even sleep when you got tired of being underwater. There was more space under the water and transparent huge windows.

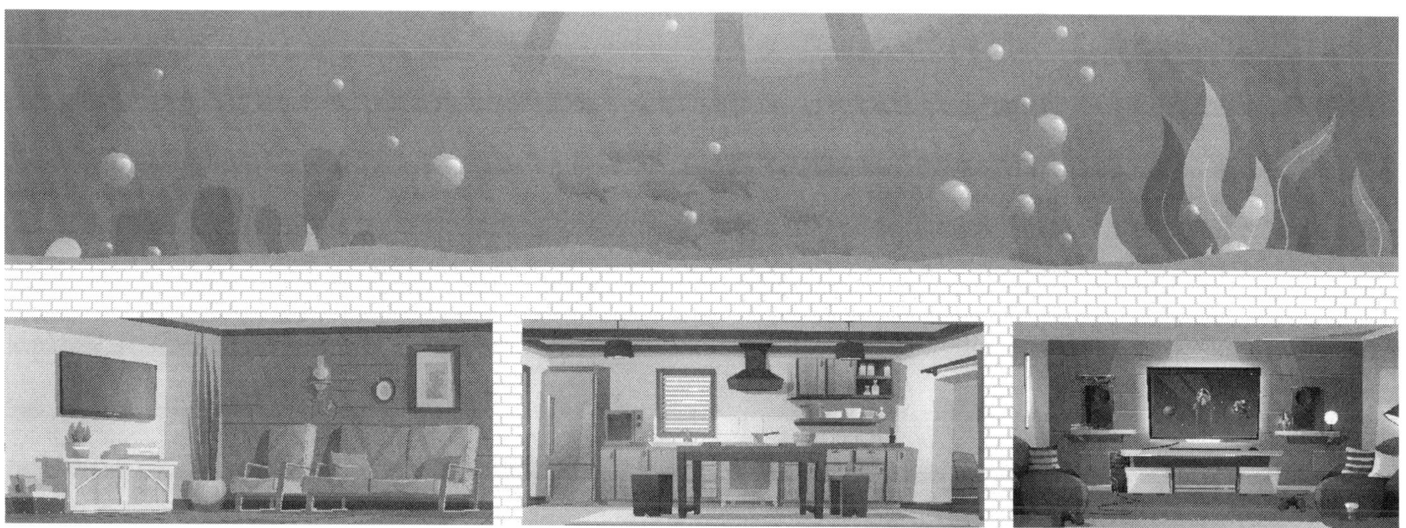

All of this reminded us of a fairy tale. We lived in this house for 2 years and were extremely satisfied. Everyone who knew us wanted to visit us and we were happy to invite them and surprise them!

The deepest dive with the use of an exoskeleton and bioengineering.

Diving to the bottom of the Mariana Trench has already become a familiar thing for us, because for several years now the tourist route for diving to the deepest point of the Submarine seamount has been operating.

However, all this happens on special bathyscaphes, which are equipment for such depths.

With the invention of a full-fledged exoskeleton, people began to use it everywhere, from work in production where you do not need to waste your strength, and you can easily lift up to 3 tons, to entertainment, like jumping from a mountain without a parachute, because the exoskeleton allows you to jump from unprecedented heights without any damage, it takes all the energy of the impact on itself.

Now the time has come for deep-sea diving, special models with a closed body and the ability to breathe underwater for 5 hours have been invented. After that, everyone suddenly disappeared from the streets and mountains, they went for a walk underwater! Why go to the park or to the beach when you can walk along the bottom of the Atlantic Ocean, and then, like on a boat, the exoskeleton will take you back to shore.

And so some smart guy decided to dive to the bottom of the Mariana Trench, and he succeeded! And mass dives began, there will not be enough people down there, there are a lot of different tourists.

The greatest digital diversion.

We all remember the insane raising of GameStop shares at the end of 2020, then it was done with the help of the company's fans who joined together on Reddit and started buying shares. They beat the market together and then showed the whole world how the shares rose from $3 to $ 80 at the peak! More than 25 times!

At the end of the 21st century, there was a new diversion that shocked millions of people.

The once great and innovative Apple company was not in the best position, for a long time its gadgets have lost their meaning with the advent of communication and interaction directly through the human brain. The shares were trading at $300 a piece, it was extremely low and everyone expected a speedy bankruptcy. However, they had an iBrain device in development, which was supposed to be a new breakthrough in meta universes and communication directly through the brain with other people.

Many fans knew this, but the market no longer believed the company. Apple desperately needed $30 billion to complete and promote its product, then on the legendary Reddit, people united again under the slogan *#SaveApple*

A huge number of people started buying shares and they went up, from the $ 300 mark they grew to an unthinkable 16 thousand dollars per share at the peak and later became worth 12 thousand dollars, which was very impressive! The growth is more than 40 times, thanks only to the fans!

I am writing this story 5 years after those events, we all know what happened after the release of iBrain. A worldwide hit, a product that radically changed our lives for the better and removed the old ways of communicating directly through the brain and literally made a computer in our head capable of realizing the most incredible and previously inaccessible tasks. This is the Apple we love!

What fantasy is capable of.

Yes, I am an ordinary lifeguard on the beach who is very lucky, because my profession, my income is enough for me in my life and I don't have a million dollars! There is only a modest 200 m2 house in Miami, a wonderful wife, children, friends and a few small loans that I plan to close in 5 years.

Saving people is my vocation, I am always vigilant and do 100% of my job, which is why I am now in charge of all rescuers in Miami and I am engaged in social activities together with creating favorable conditions for recreation on our beaches.

We started selling sand from our beaches and water. You won't believe it, but this is the bestseller on Amazon in the Gifts category. People like it and they want to give a piece of Miami to their friends and relatives. It was in this business that we managed to raise $ 10 million for donations for the construction of wells for clean water in the central regions of Africa.

"It's better not to think," I said to myself before landing on Mars.

The first tourist routes to Mars officially launched just 7 years after the first human step on the red planet.

The travel time has been reduced to 57 days, during which time guests are invited to be in hypothermic stasis and wake up immediately upon arrival on Mars. I'm flying here not only for tourist purposes, I also want to look for a piece of land. After all, recently the government of the red planet began selling the first habitable areas in the colonized part of Mars. The price bites, but you can understand the difficulties they faced. Isn't it the dream of any astronomy teacher to build a house and live on Mars?

"It's better not to think." That's exactly what I told myself before landing on Mars when we were brought out of sleep. Because it is contrary to human nature. Why Mars when there is a beautiful green Earth? I can't answer this question for myself. I only know that I can bring my share of work to the development of such difficult and distant territories, where our next generations can live and grow in the future.

Our first interplanetary transfer.

After the discovery, colonization and establishment of infrastructure on the new planet Greenspace, it has been quite a long time, at least 5 years. During this time, many Earthlings wanted to change their planet of residence, and move to a new planet. Although the path is not close, sometimes dangerous, but it does not stop people. Any earthling can get a visa, the citizenship of a new and first country called Nova is given after a continuous residence of 3 years, during which time the system collects data about your behavior, life and what you really are. After that, notifications automatically come with the message have you been given citizenship or not.

The most expensive part of the move is an interplanetary flight. The standard economy ticket includes hand luggage of 10 kg and checked baggage of 30 kg. The surcharge for the transportation of excess baggage is so high that it discouraged us from taking our favorite things, such as air skis, a floating ottoman and a statue to a smartphone.

Therefore, the move was limited to everything that we could fit into this framework. Taking the necessary things, we set off on a long journey. Arriving on the planet Greenspace, we decided to settle in the new city of Exact, where business life is actively developing.

How I assembled a space shuttle in 25 years in my backyard.

I started building a space shuttle at the age of 16. Although it could not be called an assembly process then, rather experiments and study. I spent most of the weekend in our backyard, distracted only by the family barbecue that my father liked to arrange.

My shuttle is small, about 8 meters long, 4 meters wide and 7 meters wingspan. Initially, I did not plan to try to launch it, because this requires a launch vehicle, a launch pad and a control center, or at least 1 smart dispatcher.

However, years later, I realized more and more that I would have to run it. Many people in our city already knew that I was building a shuttle. Almost every one of them was waiting for the launch day.

The day has come. Taking a permit, an old decommissioned military intercontinental missile without a shell and a shuttle, we delivered everything to the desert for launch. The installation and preparation process took 5 days of continuous operation.

The moment of truth has come, I really wanted to fly in a shuttle, but my father dissuaded me. That's why I personally didn't fly. But we had to launch the shuttle. The countdown started, all systems were normal, the launch vehicle took off confidently upwards and rushed to the lower boundary of space. 45 seconds later, we saw a bright explosion, the rocket exploded and the shuttle took the blow. We were in shock, as it turned out later, the missiles were written off for a reason, some of them could explode while in flight under high loads, that is, up, and we were just unlucky. Although it was lucky that I personally did not fly, later we all had a party and celebrated the launch. Whatever the outcome, it was still fun, and most importantly no one was injured.

The longest swim in the world in the open ocean at 10 kilometers.

The Pacific Ocean is the largest of the oceans in the world and, like any of the oceans, extremely dangerous. On the shores of Australia, a young athlete named Harvey Keitel decided to set a World record for swimming into the open ocean and back to shore, without food and water during the swim, because many swim with food and stops.

Hundreds of hours of preparation and psychological fortitude are the main things for Harvey in this difficult test.

On the day of the swim, spectators from the local town gathered. The ocean is never calm in these places and the waves are always present, this is one of the greatest difficulties, but Harvey could not be stopped, he began his swim.

After swimming 10 kilometers from the shore, he set a world record; it remained to go back. With the last of his strength, adrenaline and some wild instincts, Harvey was able to return to the shore and became the absolute champion!

How a farmer from Miami took a loan for a yacht.

Growing oranges in Miami was a profitable business until the onset of mass globalization of everything and, as a result, a rapid reduction in prices.

After several unprofitable years, one of the farmers in Miami takes a loan for a yacht, collects all the things, takes the family and sails off to an unknown destination. Surf the seas, go fishing and sell fresh fish. Discover new lands and places. Only after 8 years he returned, already a completely different person, he decided to continue his business of catching and selling fresh fish here in Miami.

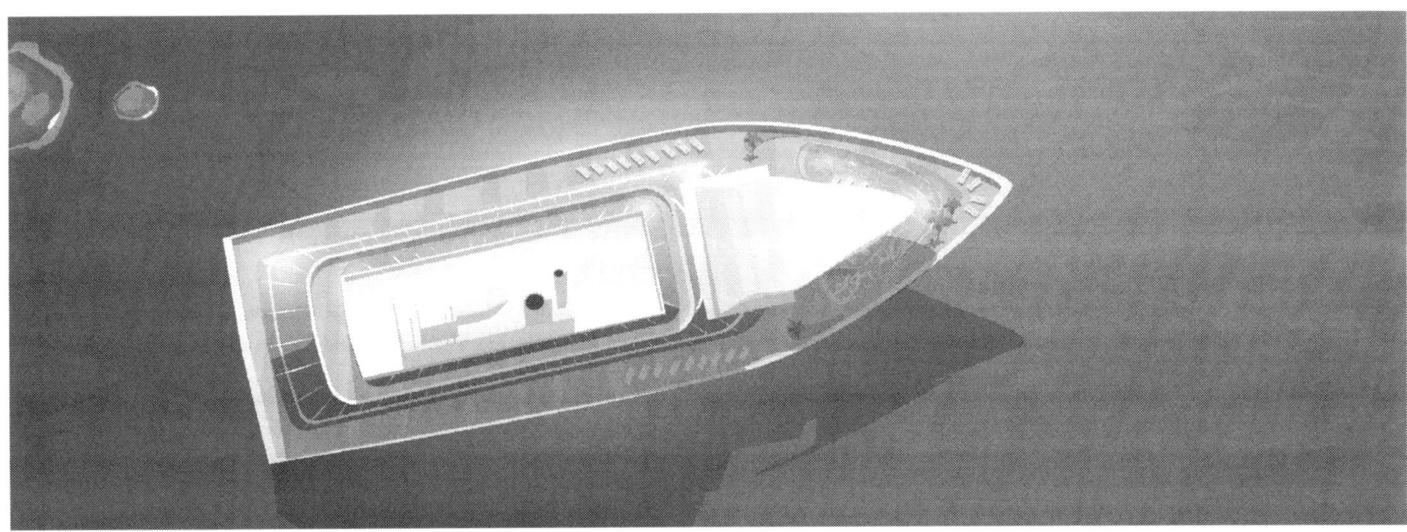

I have changed 100 jobs and different types of activities in my life.

In my youth, working on television, I did not even think about changing jobs. Every year I moved up the career ladder, received a large salary. Could afford a lot. I bought a house on credit, a car, and got a family.

After 30 years, something clicked in my head, and I decided to change my favorite job to a completely different one and chose to become a chef in a restaurant. After that, i went to the stock exchange, then worked as a bus driver, a volunteer, in a local newspaper, sold hot dogs, built garages, organized outdoor movie screenings, worked as a cashier in a store, a security guard at a factory, a handyman in a carpentry shop, a guide around his city, a bicycle seller, a cleaner in a technology company, an insurance agent, opened his own coffee shop, became an investor, installed fences, sold cars and much, much more.

All this was for the sake of a variety of work. I have changed more than 100 different types of work in my life and was extremely satisfied.

How I almost invented the teleport.

In the 22nd century, technology is ahead of time and we do not fully understand what our inventions are really capable of.

So one day I came across an interesting device. It clearly showed how it could move microparticles up to a distance of 15 cm without directly passing this distance. That is, even if there is a wall and it doesn't matter what else - the microparticle will still move 15 cm.

It seemed interesting to me, in fact a teleport, but so far in such a primitive form. I contacted the creators, came to their office and realized that the work was in full swing. I was informed that this is just a demo version of what they want to do. And it was created to support the company now, because the sales of these devices brought good money. I wanted to participate too and said that I wanted to invent a teleport together with this company. But they politely refused me and even laughed a little. There is no way to invent a teleport for a person now, they are working to move inorganic objects over long distances. Teleportation cannot be applied to organic beings and there are no solutions for this problem at the moment. Well, I tried to participate, although my help was not useful.

Everything is On request - I share my experience.

The future has come, everyone is trying to optimize it and make sure that everyone has enough. People have learned to tell themselves: "that's enough." Almost all products are manufactured according to the system "On request". A request appears, a red family crossover is manufactured and shipped at the factory. Also with almost everything to avoid situations when something will not be used or disposed of.

Books, phones, groceries, homes, work, tickets, appliances and much more - works only on the system "On request". And humanity strives to do 100% of everything and everywhere exactly on this principle.

I am an eternal sailor.

The concept of an eternal sailor is found quite often in our circles, but it has the concept of when a sailor came from a voyage and left almost immediately back. In our case, an unknown senior mechanic worked on a Chinese merchant ship for 8 years, while he never went ashore for unexplained personal reasons. Only 8 years later, when the ship was supposed to go for repairs, the sailor had to step on land, and no one saw him anymore. They say he lives in some remote northern town in Spain, looks at the ocean, and develops his small farm.

Last farm on earth for the cultivation of animal products was closed.

This has been going on since the beginning of the 21st century, slowly but surely humanity has decided that it makes no sense to keep and kill animals anymore. Meat has long been grown artificially in laboratories, with 100% identical properties. Vegetable products make cheese, milk and eggs the same as real ones. The line where the properties were different has long been crossed, and now whoever wants "real" meat buys laboratory meat, who wants only taste and texture, buys from vegetable products.

The last farm in Vietnam was officially closed. A worldwide ban on killing any animal (except for self-defense) has come into force. The new era has now definitely begun in full and in all corners of our planet.

I have been married several times, 72 times and 1 time married.

It doesn't work out the first time, that's what I tell myself every time I decide to get married again. It's even scary to say how many children I have, I'll just say that more than 20. Every time I entered into a new marriage, I did not understand whether it would work or not, I doubted. Almost always my doubts came true and something went wrong. I'm a bartender myself and not a gift, but I wanted to find the perfect wife. Once I even decided to change my orientation and got married. It didn't work out either. Now I have been divorced 73 times and am looking for a new partner.

How Steve Gates opened factory for the production of calculators.

Steve Gates is an interesting guy, he was always fascinated by numbers and he didn't understand why calculators are so boring and don't allow you to do big calculations. Therefore, at the age of 21, he decided to create his own company for the production of super-productive nano calculators.

"Door-Pear" is the name chosen for the future company. Things gradually went up and today these calculators are considered the most advanced, reliable and high-quality.

My brother and I built a 28-storey residential building.

The dream of building our own apartment building led us to local bankers, and later to investors, but they all insisted that such a high-rise was not needed in our small town and we did not receive funding for full-scale construction. My brother and I had other thoughts on this matter, we believed that in just some 20 years our city, by the big river, would be in great demand. After all, warm and pleasant places in our country are limited, and our tidbit has not yet been mastered and looked after by other people.

Therefore, after selling everything that is possible and adding personal funds, we purchased 2 hectares of land on the outskirts of the city, of which 1 hectare will go under public spaces and a park. The remaining 1 hectare will be used for the construction of our house.

We started construction in 2026 and completed it in 2058, but the sale of the first premises and the settlement of people was already in 2046, we spent the remaining 12 years completing the upper floors and finishing works. After all, we did everything ourselves, with the help of rented equipment, we performed complex work, the rest with our own hands. 182 apartments and developed infrastructure around. Now this is our main asset, because our city has grown more than 15 times during this time! And once it was the outskirts, and now it is part of the city and almost the center.

How I earned my first billion on beetroot chips.

Beetroot chips, what could be better for a snack on a hike when you don't want to cook or on vacation?

I also thought so and started my eco-business for the production of beet chips with gentle drying up to 45 °C. At the same time, all trace elements are preserved and the product remains RAW.

There were more customers, we began to expand and also engaged in: pastilles, vegetable bread, nanoproducts of rapid saturation, mountain water from the purest sources and many others.

After 11 years, we have become the number one manufacturer of ECO-products in North America, and we continue to delight our customers with high-quality and innovative products.

Hijack a billionaire's helicopter.

How to hijack a helicopter worth $4.5 million? First of all, you need to gain trust. This is exactly what an unknown gardener in Florida did, who got a job with a billionaire through the manager of a large management company.

Pretending to be a calm gardener, he never caused problems, over time they began to trust him even more than just a garden, he took tools himself, had access to the house, and was in good standing.

However, one day everything turned upside down, at night everyone woke up from a loud helicopter takeoff, no one understood anything and the owner of the house immediately called the police. However, it was too late, the helicopter flew off in an unknown direction and disappeared from radar, as it most likely flew over the nearest mountains.

An ordinary gardener turned out to be a thoughtful hijacker who carefully thought everything through to the smallest detail and hijacked a helicopter in just a few minutes.

Two microprocessor manufacturing factories opposite each other.

In modern society, microprocessors have begun to fade into the background. If earlier it was one of the most important areas of technology development, now everything has changed. Thanks to the use of computing power in cloud mode, it became unnecessary to have powerful microprocessors at home.

However, they are still in demand, and the only question is the price. That is why there are two independent manufacturers of microprocessors in our holding, these are the main players and they are in fierce competition among themselves for the cost of microprocessors of the 2100 Standard. This standard describes the requirements that are sufficient for any tasks performed by an individual related to work or personal affairs. There is no point in making it more productive at the moment, because this is an excessive "power" that will not be used.

The science fiction writer became an actor and playwright.

The writer became an actor. Why would he do that?

Richard Brooks is a famous science fiction writer from the suburbs of London. His most famous books: "Embrace" and "Life after" are world bestsellers that brought him fame and popularity.

For more than 2 years, the author has not published new books, when, as before, he pleased his readers every six months. Many thought that this was due to the writing of an extremely complex and great book. However, everything turned out to be simpler.

After conducting our own investigation in the Texas newspaper, we found out that Richard Brooks has been working as an actor and playwright for 6 months and has already participated in 2 productions.

The writer himself, and now an actor, does not comment on this, but his close friend said that Richard did everything he wanted in the book business and now just wants to be an actor, he does not need new fame in this image, so the press now knows so little about his current life.

We can only wish you happiness and thank you for the incredible books that have forever changed our understanding of fiction.

Michael got rid of the phone and the Internet more than 10 years ago.

Michael Denessi, a famous volleyball player, coach and just a good person. Why did we all forget about him after the 2036 Olympics?

Michael stayed to live in his hometown, he only radically changed his lifestyle. Now he lives without a phone and Internet. You can only communicate and meet him live. He is not hiding and teaches at a local high school. An unusual fate, a person completely disappeared from the public's field of view only due to the fact that he stopped using the Internet and the phone.

I built the most popular beach in my city.

My city suffers from poor ecology, the local landfill in the suburbs stretches along a beautiful lake that people don't want to go to now.

It took a year to solve this problem, a bunch of letters, videos, a public protest, and only after that the local authorities decided to remove the landfill and build a recycling plant far from the city.

I applied for the lease of this land, no one wanted to take it up because there was a lot of work ahead and it's not a fact that people will go there. We gathered with friends, volunteers came, local entrepreneurs supported us financially, someone even came himself. We started our work on the improvement of this territory, planted a lawn, made benches, tents, and opened two cafes. It also became easier to get here because the local bus added a stop called "lake".

Six months later, there were already a lot of people on the beach, whole crowds, I would say. There is no trace of the former landfill.

The first scientific expedition to the center of Antarctica.

The first scientific expedition to the center of Antarctica under an incredibly thick layer of ice is a major state project that is comparable in complexity to a flight to the moon.

The most difficult thing is to get under 2.5 kilometers of ice. Such a point was chosen for the dive. The map of Antarctica without ice has been published for a long time, starting with Bedmap1, later a more detailed map of Antarctica Bedmap2 and finally the most detailed thorough map of Bedmap3. Every mountain, every gorge, relief and all the features of this unknown continent were completely mapped.

A revolutionary device is the ultra-impassable U-Boat Worx bathyscaphe, together with a laser ground installation that will make a sufficient hole in depth and diameter for the expedition to go to the very bottom.

After the first human foot set foot on the land of Antarctica under a layer of ice, it was clear that these were once beautiful lands, but nature ordered otherwise and this continent was carried to the south pole, which caused the appearance of glaciers. The exploration of the bottom took 16 hours, that was how long it was before the need to return to the top. Rock specimens were taken at the bottom, the first conclusions made it clear that life once flourished here, several remains of previously unknown dinosaurs were found, and various minerals.

How I opened my first restaurant. In Mount Everest.

I decided to open my first restaurant right in Mount Everest. It is in it. At an altitude of 2 kilometers above sea level there is a small village near Mount Everest, tourists often come there and this place was chosen for the restaurant. The local authorities allowed about 100 m2 to be hollowed out in the mountain to create a restaurant in the mountain. Part of it was there, the kitchen was moved to a separate building next to the restaurant. Only our guests were sitting in the mountain.

The restaurant quickly became the most famous in these circles and everyone who comes to Everest should visit here, because he will not see this anywhere else.

My fig plantation on the southern coast of the Crimean peninsula.

The southern coast of the Crimean peninsula occupies a strip of the Black Sea coast on the southern slope of the Main Ridge of the Crimean Mountains from Cape Aya in the west to the Karadag massif in the east with a length of about 150-180 km and a width of 2-12 km. This is an amazing place in the northern part of the Black Sea. Pomegranates, kiwi, persimmon, figs and many other fruits, vegetables and berries grow here.

My fig plantation is located above the town of Partenit, near the Bear Mountain in the town of Gurzuf. Here I inherited from my grandfather 4 hectares of fertile land together with fig trees.

My family lives not far from here, we take care of our trees and really appreciate each of them.

Every summer in the middle of August, all our extended family and friends begin the seasonal fig harvest. This is one of the most wonderful times of the year when everyone can get together and do useful work. After assembly, we eat part of it right away, dry part and save it for autumn and winter, put another part up for sale, they take it all from us at once.

How a single one-day hike in the mountains lasted two months.

Hiking in the mountains can be a fun walk if it's for 1 day, or become a real challenge in the mountains of Alaska if something goes wrong.

In my case, it was the second option. It's all about the hungry local wolf pack. Going down the mountain, I found that someone else was following me. Steals carefully and slowly. Every time I fell asleep near the campfire, I felt someone else, footsteps, breathing, and barking. It became clear that a wolf pack was following me, only a fire and a gun with 2 cartridges could save me. The wolves were thin, their ribs stuck out and it was unclear how they moved, and did not fall into snowdrifts.

I had to light a fire more and more often to scare away hungry animals, each time their arrogance was higher and they came closer and closer.

There were about 4 days left to go to the settlement, but they were delayed for 2 months due to severe frosts and the inability to go further because of wolves.

I got there and survived, but the experience that I managed to experience now is even scary to remember.

All the plants of the world are in my garden.

Plants, trees, shrubs, flowers, grass and foliage - all this gives harmony to my space, brings pleasure and relaxation.

My garden is located in the vicinity of Altamura, Italy. I am 62 years old, I have already retired after working as a school geography teacher for most of my life. Now I collect the rarest and most unusual plants in the world.

I have 1.5 hectares of land and 6 greenhouses at my disposal. To date, I have more than 350 thousand plant species from all over the world. However, new discoveries are still happening and my collection is always replenished and open to new things. Nevertheless, the Guinness Book of Records recognized that my garden had all the plants known to date and was the largest in terms of the number of plants in one place.

My goal was not to get into this book at all, I just collected all the plants of the World and wanted to study them more. Anyone can come to me and study all these plants. Every week a group of local school children goes to my volunteer work and helps to take care of the garden.

I am the owner of a safari park.

The former director of the state zoo, decided to realize his passion for wild animals and open his own safari park with lions.

A place was chosen for a long time and in the end it was chosen, a huge territory of more than 30 hectares where 60 lions, 40 tigers, as well as hundreds of other small animals now live freely.

The main business card of the park is lions, and the founder, because he communicates with them directly, strokes, feeds with his hands, knows absolutely everything about everyone. It's not an easy job, but it's his. After all, he is not here for the position of director, but for the development of his business.

I don't have a birthday and that's why.

A leap year contains an additional 1 day, February 29, to adjust the time offset each year by 6 hours.

In the future, due to global warming, displacement continued and 20 minutes were added. It would seem a little, but scientists had to add another 1 day, February 30, only not once every 4 years, but once every 72 years. And it was on this first officially added day that I was born.

Now I am 29 years old and officially my next birthday should be when I am 72 years old, I will look forward to it.

Why you can't live on your island for a long time.

Many people dream of buying their own island. If once it was possible only by being at least a millionaire, now the requirements have increased and you need to be at least a billionaire or be born into a family where there is already an island.

The reason is the worldwide strong rise in prices for real estate and, most importantly, land. Now there are already some settlements in any desert or on any mountain, and not because they like it there, but because there is still available land there. People have already begun to drain parts of the seas and lakes, just to add land to their place and start using it.

Therefore, ownership of the island became available only to a select few. And one of them, the "modern Robinson Crusoe", told what it's like to live permanently on the island and why you can't do it for a long time.

To come to rest or to live permanently are different things. When you have the second one, you realize that you are in a golden prison. Everything is beautiful, but there is only a boundless ocean around and it takes 2 hours to fly to the nearest mainland. Even claustrophobia can easily develop. That's why I recommend living with significant breaks. For example, a month after a month. This is the most successful option. The second of the disadvantages is the lack of diversity in food. Most of the diet becomes marine products, because shipping specifically to our island is extremely costly and difficult, there are islands with the best location, but presidents live there at least, ordinary billionaires have to buy islands in the farthest parts of the Pacific Ocean.

I lived in three centuries.

From about the age of 18, my dream was to live in three centuries. I was lucky and I was born in 1998, respectively, I lived in the 20th century for two years. Then the main part of my life took place in the 21st century. And here I decided to try different types of nutrition and lifestyle in order to increase life expectancy, although on the other hand, in youth there is stress from work and the need to achieve success, but the nutrition still helped. It seemed interesting to me raw food, or fruit eating, as a temporary diet helps to restore the body and give vigor, the main thing is high-quality fruits.

Having lived to my 103rd birthday, I officially lived 1 year in the 22nd century and fulfilled my goal. Now I am writing my book of memories and sharing my experiences with future generations. There are things that do not change and remain the same regardless of technology and the situation in the world.

How an artist near the sea painted one picture all his life.

It's a strange thing to draw one picture all my life, but for me it's more than a hobby, it's a ritual. Our house is located 3 kilometers from the sea on the mountain. Every evening I go to our garden under a canopy, from where an amazing view of the sea opens. There is also my canvas of 2 by 8 meters on which I have been painting a huge landscape of the sea for more than 20 years. It is important for me to convey the full depth, every millimeter and all details must be perfect and absolute. I'm not in a hurry, the main thing for me is to make a perfect picture of my life.

Kings of the land.

Kings of the land.

This is the only way to call a famous English family that has the largest amount of land in personal possession in the whole world. Having conducted our independent investigation, we can state that the family is engaged in light industry, has its own cotton and chocolate factories, and invests all funds in the purchase of land with further long-term leases.

1,240 hectares, that's how many around the world but mostly in Texas, belong to an unknown English family.

Work in Russia's secret gold storage.

It is strictly forbidden to talk about such an experience and you will never know my real name, where I came from, in which particular gold depository I worked, when and how much.

All details about me are excluded. I anonymously tell you about my work experience and how everything works.

The first thing that catches your eye after hiring is an inexplicable feeling that we are not in the 21st century, but in the middle of the 20th century. Everything works and is arranged as it was before under the Soviet Union. People don't even seem to have changed since those times. Everything is pretty strict and tough.

The storage is located in one of the mountains in Siberia, where one of the largest gold storage facilities in all of Russia has been masked extremely seriously. Not only gold is stored here, but also cash from different countries of the world, valuable paintings and books of antiquity, various exhibits and even a Neanderthal skeleton. There is a secret special section, only the president has access to it, and I do not know what is stored there.

The whole building is located on 3 levels, a railway is laid, there is also a small runway for summer time.

The amount of gold that is stored here is measured in thousands of tons, to be more precise, about two thousand tons. This is a large part of Russia's gold.

The job is highly paid but stressful, which is why I quit and no longer plan to work in such places.

I lived 8 years on the ISS.

The flight to the International Space Station was accompanied by a child's expectation of a miracle, because a flight into space and especially life at such a station is a once-in-a-lifetime adventure.

The most difficult thing that happens even before the flight, this is the selection for the team that will fly to the ISS. Hundreds of physical and psychological tests of endurance and competence take place here. When you get the cherished decision to fly on the ISS, you become the happiest person on Earth! That's exactly what happened to me. I will not even be able to describe the fullness of joy and delight from receiving just one paper that I am flying to the ISS.

After starting life on the ISS, your working day from Monday to Saturday brings only pleasure and scientific interest. Our main task is to conduct scientific experiments that are impossible on Earth, as well as station maintenance.

After 8 years of such a life, I missed the feeling of the ground under my feet quite a lot. I've been used to this kind of life for a long time, but looking at the Earth every day from my porthole, I understand that this is my home and I want to come back.

At the end of my 8-year contract, I returned home. The first thing I did was take a deep breath and say to myself "I'm home."

Meta universes.

More than 5 years have passed since the appearance of full-fledged Meta universes. During this time, almost every user of ordinary social networks has tried or switched to the Meta universe.

I share my 3-year experience, during this time I managed to build and sell 7 Meta houses, own 3 hectares of land in Meta Miami and continue to develop. I perceive it all as a serious second or even first life. After all, in the real world it is much more difficult to achieve this, in the Meta World it is still available to almost everyone who is ready to work.

My day starts with a cup of coffee, then I get ready and put on my Meta Glasses. I turn on the Meta World in them and go to work in it. At the same time, the body remains motionless at will and everything is controlled only by thought. If there is space and it is safe, then you can control your real body. In this mode, sensors will be enabled to protect against accidental possible damage in the real world.

For the eyes, glasses do not strain and do not spoil vision.

Meta universe is a breakthrough that allows even more people to become happy. This World is a complete copy of the map of our real world. The money earned in the Meta universe also works in our real world. Laws, rights, physics and much more are made for a realistic copy of our planet. There are only a few "improvements" but in general it is a copy.

Entertainment without laws and physics is available in a special mode, the consequences in it do not affect anything.

My company is "House on Request".

People have long learned to print books on request when there is no need to make large print runs, and printing is done at the moment when a person orders a book.

Now almost everything works on the "on request" system, from clothes to phones and products in the store. We are close to getting rid of overproduction and having an ideal life cycle where everything is applicable, when it is needed and to whom it is needed and how it is needed.

Construction went on with slow but confident steps, there were attempts to make houses "on request", but it turned out to be not convenient or not of high quality.

After the main and largest Open company decided to undertake construction on request, everything changed.

It became possible to use 3d visualization projection to think over your home based on ready-made proven projects or to implement your project in which all the necessary norms and requirements will be taken into account automatically.

After the project is created, artificial intelligence analyzes it together with the company manager and gives advice as needed, after the final approval, the formalities are solved, where, when. Payment is made and at the same moment special airships take off that begin to build a house on your site on request.

The process guarantees 100% accuracy, quality and compliance with all standards. The service life of houses on request is three times higher compared to ordinary houses. At the same time, the cost is 1.5 times lower! Houses will become even more affordable, more durable, more reliable and more convenient to order and build. Robots are able to build a house of 200 m2 fully ready for occupancy in just 2 weeks. They work around the clock, do not know how to rest, and work smoothly and accurately. They can be built literally everywhere, even under water, but we don't live there yet.

Meat without meat, gold without gold.

It all started back in ancient times, with the first replacement of heavy round stones (the money of those times) with silver and gold coins. Later, the coins were replaced with receipts from moneylenders that had these coins, because it was hard to carry a bunch of coins with you. These receipts in the 20th-21st century were called money. Until 1971, the dollar was pegged to gold, in fact, at any time it was possible to exchange a dollar for a fixed amount of gold. The dollar was a receipt that I had some amount of real gold. Later it was canceled and the dollar itself became a value and it became possible to print it as much as you like.

This simple example shows the current state of most things. Meat on the shelves consists of vegetable ingredients or grown in the laboratory without killing animals. Alcohol is a safe soluble powder in water that has the same relaxation but without unpleasant consequences or harm to the body. Gold bullion can only be bought as a digital unit. Physical bullion has been banned for sale and is stored in the reserves of the state. Only jewelry of 585 gold samples remained. Cash no longer exists, only digital units. There are no physical documents either. Humanity digitizes everything that is possible and gets rid of the original.

We ordered a "House on Request".

House on Request for 2 weeks.

Such an advertisement was launched by the Open company with the release of its ultramodern innovative House on Request.

In general, we already planned to build a house with the help of a building company using the old methods with minimal use of robots. But we decided to be one of the first to order a House on Request.

At first, we coordinated everything with artificial intelligence, and the manager did not even communicate with us, everything could be solved without him. After that, we paid and indicated when and where to start. After 20 minutes, the robots arrived at our site and began a silent revolutionary construction, which could be watched by a 3D camera.

After only 14 days, our house was completely ready, all the furniture, appliances and even our things, which the robot took away, were delivered and laid out in the house.

We ate, watched a movie and went to bed. The next day we started as if nothing had happened and immediately got down to business. The robot laid out things as it were in our past housing, taking into account our preferences and their calculations.

Revolution, 1.5 times cheaper, 100 times better and otherwise. This has never happened before in the experience of mankind. We are happy with our 280 m2 house in Los Angeles.

The whole life in rented housing around the world.

I personally don't like owning anything, my grandfather was a hippie, I probably inherited it from him and I myself look like a long-forgotten subculture.

Therefore, I live in very different conditions, with different people, and my work is also different. I don't expect much from life and I like to just live and act right now according to the situation, maybe it's not responsible, but I chose this lifestyle, outdated, but I'm one of the few who follows such simple rules.

My partner and I have opened a family restaurant.

Thinking about where to open our family restaurant together with my partner, we decided that the best idea was to buy a medium-sized ship, like a barge, and place a restaurant on it. Place it in the middle of the Mediterranean Sea, give mass advertising throughout Europe and deliver visitors free of charge by helicopter from anywhere in Europe. It sounds crazy, but we did it. Now we have crowds of tourists who just want to stay in the middle of the Mediterranean Sea, where the ship is struggling with waves and wind every second. Have a delicious meal in the restaurant and if you want to stay overnight in our cabins, where we have made a hotel.

You can also explore the seabed with the help of the latest bathyscaphe capable of diving to the very bottom of the Mediterranean Sea, 5121 meters. After all, we are standing near a deep-water trough in the southern part of Greece. The capacity of the bathyscaphe is 9 tourists and 1 operator.

In search of treasures.

Somewhere at the bottom of the Black Sea lies the legendary ship Black Prince, the keeper of the looted treasures of the 18th century. It was this ship that became our goal with my brother.

After collecting all the equipment and renting a bathyscaphe, we went on a treasure hunt. With the help of the latest locator and modern bottom scanning, we searched day and night for a sunken ship in the Black Sea.

After 8 days of searching, we came across only old fishing boats and human garbage. We didn't give up and continued our search. On the 9th day we found some wreckage of an ancient ship, but it turned out to be a ship of the Romans, who once drowned here. Unfortunately, we did not find any valuable treasures, but this adventure will be remembered by my brother and me forever. Maybe one day we will come back and luck will smile on us and we will find the mysterious ship Black Prince.

The longest hitchhiking trip.

Starting my hitchhiking trip in Portugal, I got to the Kamchatka Peninsula, in the northeastern part of Russia.

The trip took me 4 months during which I managed to visit every country on my way, meet dozens of kind and sympathetic people, live different lives, see different cultures and get to such a cold and remote place as the Kamchatka Peninsula. An adventure that I will never forget!

My eco-house is made of recycled garbage.

I built my eco-house together with my father and friends. Its main feature is that most of the materials consist of recycled garbage.

This became available quite a long time ago, now materials, raw materials and things can serve more than once or twice, they are processed and something else is done. This principle is laid down in our modern society. Additionally, the "on request" system helps a lot. Where all production and provision of services work only when it is needed and in the quantity that is needed.

99% of my house is former garbage. Now it has been redesigned and is again usable. The service life of my house is 100 years, after which it will also be automatically disposed of and other houses or other goods will be made from it. It depends on what will be needed.

Now garbage is not associated with something old, but on the contrary with the material for future goods, with our belongings and houses. Today 99% of everything can be recycled. The 1% we are fighting are extremely complex chemicals that still have to be used, but to a lesser extent. According to forecasts, in 7 years we will be able to recycle 100% of everything related to humans.

Life on the edge of the earth - literally.

My house is on the edge of the earth, and this is not a metaphor, but a reality.

After the colonization of the Moon, Mars and the exoplanet Greenspace, people also began to populate strange space objects. We found that there are huge plates that act as satellites for some planets, and one of them had a fully developed life. These are primitive forms, but the main thing is that there is air here, the plate is safe and you can live on it even without a spacesuit, unlike the Moon and Mars.

It was on such a plate called Plaka that I and my group of researchers were sent for colonization.

My house is literally located 150 meters from the cliff of the plate, in fact it is impossible to fall there. Since there is almost terrestrial gravity and, accordingly, I will only change my position and go further, but I will already feel that I am walking sideways due to the fact that I am used to walking only on a flat surface.

From the outside, it looks like a cliff into the cosmic abyss, in reality, the entire plate can be bypassed from all sides. Dimensions: width 250 kilometers, height 45 kilometers and length 1700 kilometers.

I have 27 children.

I am 108 years old, I have lived in three centuries: 20th century, 21st century and 22nd century, born in 1995.

It so happened that I have 27 children, from beloved wives at different times. I didn't think there would be so many, but it just so happened.

Having such a big family is a great happiness, the main thing is to remember everyone. I try to repeat the names of my children, grandchildren and great-grandchildren every day, as well as look at their photos. This is my daily memory workout before breakfast.

When we gather with the whole family, we have to do it in the gym and only relatives come, they can't take their friends, otherwise we just won't fit. Every year we gather for my birthday, Thanksgiving and Christmas.

Also, almost every day someone from a relative has a birthday, I have it all written down and I always congratulate everyone from the very morning.

How humanity settled distant exoplanets.

After the settlement of the first exoplanet, humanity began to look for new planets, because now the race has gone for space exploration and becoming a full-fledged interplanetary species.

After careful searches and analyses for several years, scientists have come to the conclusion that the nearest exoplanets are 1400 years away from us in continuous flight at the maximum speed available today.

Hypothermic stasis allowed people to be immersed in a long sleep with a slowing of metabolism, and it was this crucial technology that allowed us to master Greenspace. However, there was a significant limitation, although the person was in a dream, the metabolism and the aging process still went on, but at a rate of 10% of normal. 1400 years is too much and even if you send babies, they need to live 140 years in flight to enter a new planet.

We had to resort to Plan B. A team of 22-year-olds trained 20 men and 20 women to conceive children during the flight and taught them everything necessary to keep themselves in a dream for as long as possible, but later died of their own death. The children also had to teach their children already. They, in turn, also had to recreate the younger generation, which will be the main future colonization. At the same time, the penultimate generation will also enter the planet and will be managers in old age.

And so it happened. To master a distant planet, three generations of people had to die in space. Two of them were born there at once and have never seen anything other than a spaceship. Such a sacrifice was made for the sake of interplanetary settlement. The new planet was named: Tharros.

Intergalactic super internet.

Communication between exoplanets: Greenspace, Tharros and our home planet Earth, has become extremely difficult due to large delays. So one message from Earth to Greenspace goes for about 79 years. It's incredibly long. From Greenspace to Tharros is 700 years old. Messages go 2 times faster than our fastest ship.

To solve this problem, it took all the human intelligence on the entire planet Earth. And a solution has been found, the message can be accelerated, but it will still be very, very long.

Therefore, they must be teleported in a special encrypted form using hydrogen atoms. Teleportation is no longer a fairy tale, however, it is only available for microparticles. So, with the help of the next flights, humanity has installed special teleport installations on all human habitats in space, including ships that are regularly in flight.

Then it turned out to translate the cipher of hydrogen atoms into a language that could describe the Internet. And you won't believe it, thus the intergalactic super Internet became available. The cipher of hydrogen atoms, ultra-high-speed Internet data transmission installations on Earth and the installation of special data teleports (microparticles) at every human habitat in space. This is how we can describe how we were able to "cheat" the speed of light and in fact overcome it, because now we communicate between planets online with a delay of 0.0000000001 seconds and even want to reduce it. The fastest internet in the whole cosmos!

Comparison of exoplanets with Earth.

	Earth	Greenspace	Plaka	Tharros
Average cost of living per month	2500,00$	2900,00$	3200,00$	2700,00$
Number of people	19 billion	less than 100 million	less than 100 thousand	less than 5 thousand
Square	510 million km^2	235 billion km^2	8,6 million km^2	280 million km^2
Safety	High	High where people live, the rest is not fully explored	Average due to the irregular shape of the planet	An unexplored planet
Wildlife	All parts are inhabited, less than 3% nature	More than 99% wildlife	More than 99% wildlife	More than 99% wildlife
How many years has humanity been living	7 million years	About 30 years	About 5 years	About 3 years

Trillions of hectares of incomparable land for life.

Trillions of hectares of incomparable, fertile, rich and very comfortable land for life on our new planet Greenspace. The climate is from subtropical to tropical. In some places there are colder zones, but we haven't got there yet. As we explore new lands, we understand how much diversity and abundance of life there is here. Most of the species of flora and fauna were not known to us before and there is a huge amount of work to be done to study and adapt to a new place. There are two mega continents on the planet and hundreds of thousands (if not more) of small islands, ranging in size from a football field to Italy. All this will need to be studied for an infinite amount of time in the future. Now, everyone who moves to a new planet is supposed to have their own 1 hectare of land, 1 standard house "on request" and 1 universal air-sea-land vehicle.

There are enough people willing to move and the main thing is that there are a lot of places here, even if all earthlings want to move and give each child and adult 1 hectare of land, there will still be an unthinkable 9 trillion 481 billion hectares of land (14 trillion hectares are occupied by seas and oceans)!

It is for this reason that the artificial intelligence of the planet Greenspace actively encourages humanity to populate this planet. There are bonuses from the state for each child. This planet will be enough for a person for hundreds of thousands of years ahead of active settlement and study.

The return of small businesses.

A lot has changed since artificial intelligence came and entered our lives. If not almost everything.

For example, one of the most serious changes is the introduction of artificial intelligence in all companies in the world. Jobs have been preserved. Artificial intelligence does not interfere in the decision-making process and business development of each company. Artificial intelligence controls legality and security for end users. It simplifies life because it immediately shows what standards to observe, how to build factories correctly, and what should be taken into account when producing food.

The drastic change forced more than half of the dubious or even criminal companies to leave. You can't work in the shadows anymore. All companies, everywhere and always under supervision, for the safety of all people.

Such a change stimulated people to develop small businesses, because tax incentives were in effect for them, large companies were restricted in monopolies, and the market opened up to new small and completely different players. It has become fashionable again to do a small family business. After all, it was possible to earn about as much as the owner of Amazon earns. All for reasons of progressive taxes and serious requirements for large companies where profits were more evenly distributed.

It doesn't matter if you are an Amazon owner or a domestic worker, both can earn a decent living. The word "enough" has become a new trend. The more a person wanted beyond "enough", the harder and more difficult it was to achieve. Taxes could easily reach 99.9%! Out of $1 billion a year, there could be $1 million a year left. When, as a hardworking carpenter, he could earn about 100 thousand dollars a year a year and his taxes would be only 1%.

First meta virtual shopping center.

Meta Shopping center is the latest development of Open company. Lie down, turn on iBrain, dive into the meta universe. Here is a "real" full-size meta shopping center. 3 floors, any shops, all sizes and all products are always available (because they are made "on request").

You walk around the mall, look at goods, measure them, take products, taste them if necessary (a certain signal goes to your receptors that indicates exactly this taste).

We took everything we needed, paid, talked with friends and disconnected. Within 30 minutes, the drone delivered everything you ordered from the meta shopping center to your home.

You can connect to both the public "world" and the personal one, where no one will see you.

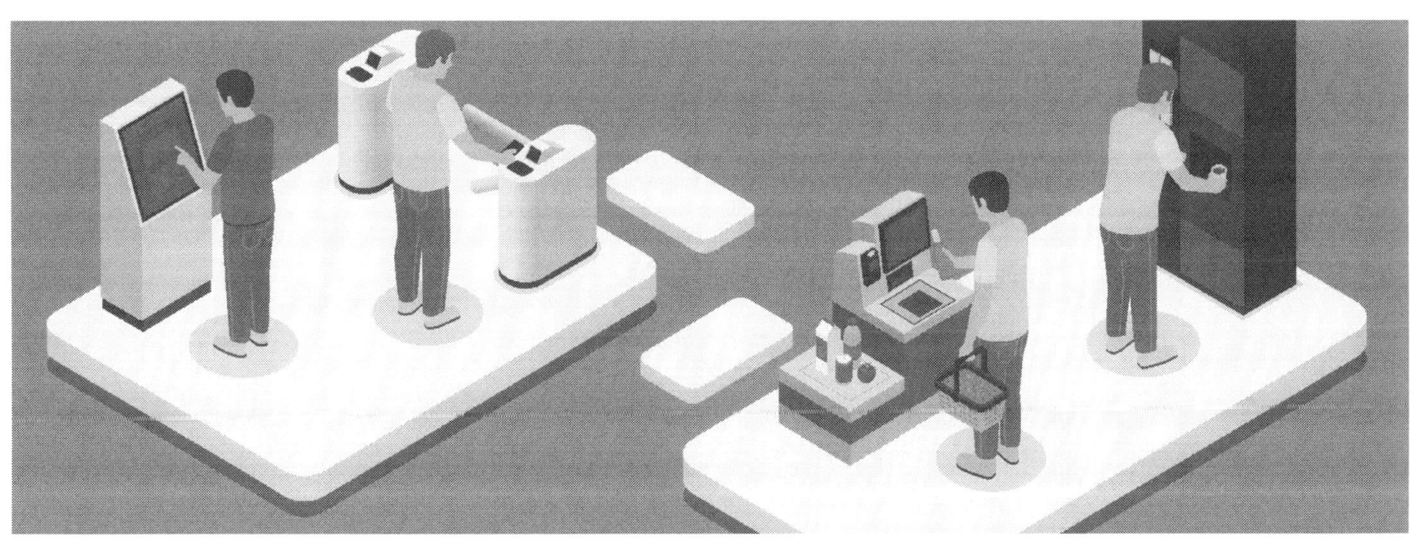

Meta World.

After opening the Meta World, I realized that I needed to invest all my available funds in it because of its laws.

Meta World was officially approved by the state, and later by artificial intelligence, repeats an exact copy of the planet Earth with the exception of any traces of man. That is, this Land on which there were no people yet. Everything was recreated extremely accurately and reliably. Every centimeter repeated the Earth and was not a distinctive copy. At the same time, it was in this World that the same laws worked as in the real world and even the laws of physics (although they could be circumvented here).

All this was created for the harmonious unhurried development of this Meta World.

Immediately after the opening, I began to buy land from the state in various promising areas of the Earth in the future. I also bought 19 islands and at the end of the first 3 years I officially became the largest landowner in the whole world. Meta World.

Self-employed people.

After the arrival of artificial intelligence, it became fashionable to be a self-employed person. This was most encouraged. There were, of course, scientific centers, research and large-scale projects where hundreds of people united. But mostly still self-employed people occupied most of the people.

Artificial intelligence gave reliability for centuries, all the weapons of all countries were destroyed and banned. The laws were 100% respected, because control was everywhere and always. With such reliability of tomorrow, it has become not fashionable to invest in other people's companies, it has become fashionable to invest in your business, in your development.

After all, you know for sure that your business will remain, if something happens to you, a relative or another person will come to your place, and artificial intelligence will settle this issue and pay the value of the business and assets at the market price. At any moment, everyone may want to sell their business and they will receive money instantly, if their business is of value, of course.

Everyone already has houses, rent as such has disappeared, only hotels for temporary accommodation remain. Investments have changed the vector from huge foreign corporations to their own small business.

We lacked land in the 24th century.

It was the 24th century, humanity has long been an interplanetary species, so there is so much earth on the exoplanet Greenspace that it will not be populated entirely in the next few hundred thousand years.

However, things are different on the native planet Earth. Things have changed a lot in the last 200 years. The earth became a factory for other planets on which they did not want to manufacture rockets, teleports and other difficult things. There are too many people on Earth, at the moment there are about 60 billion people. The limit at the same time was about 43 billion, when people could comfortably distribute evenly on Earth. Unfortunately, people do not want to be evenly distributed, many are drawn closer to the tropics, and few people want to live in Siberia. Now where the heat is guaranteed there are crowds of people, huge prices and everything is against staying here. There are preferential programs in Siberia, there are still places, but quite a lot of people are already coming.

We had to "get" new lands. To do this, with the help of space lasers and parallel drying of water, the whole country of Greenland, an additional 1,850 thousand km2, was completely extracted from under the ice. This was enough for the resettlement of 3 billion people.

Artificial islands were built in the oceans, where a wealthy middle class of 1 billion people settled. Free tickets to move to the planet Greenspace have also done their job and more than 5 billion people have left Earth in 10 years.

Additionally, the shores of Antarctica were also extracted as well as those of Greenland earlier. This has provided new housing for more than 3 billion people. Thus, we were gradually able to solve the issue of overpopulation, more than 1 child in the family cannot be had for free now, it will cost the family expensively. On the contrary, there is a lot of space on Greenspace and they try to send as many earthlings there as possible.

Artificial intelligence is everywhere.

For whom paradise, and for whom it was better before.

After the introduction of artificial intelligence into our lives, everything has changed. For the first time, laws began to work 100% for the development of humanity and security. Never before have we come across such an advanced and instant legal system. Any documents, issues and disputes must be resolved as quickly, efficiently and honestly as possible.

People are no longer afraid. The weapons are gone, the police are gone (instead there are patrol robots, they will perform any of the tasks many times better than a human).

Each person is engaged in his own business, works for a company or has opened his own family business. The level of happiness and security is the highest for the entire existence of people. The mortality rate is also the lowest.

Artificial intelligence has changed us forever and we will not be the same.

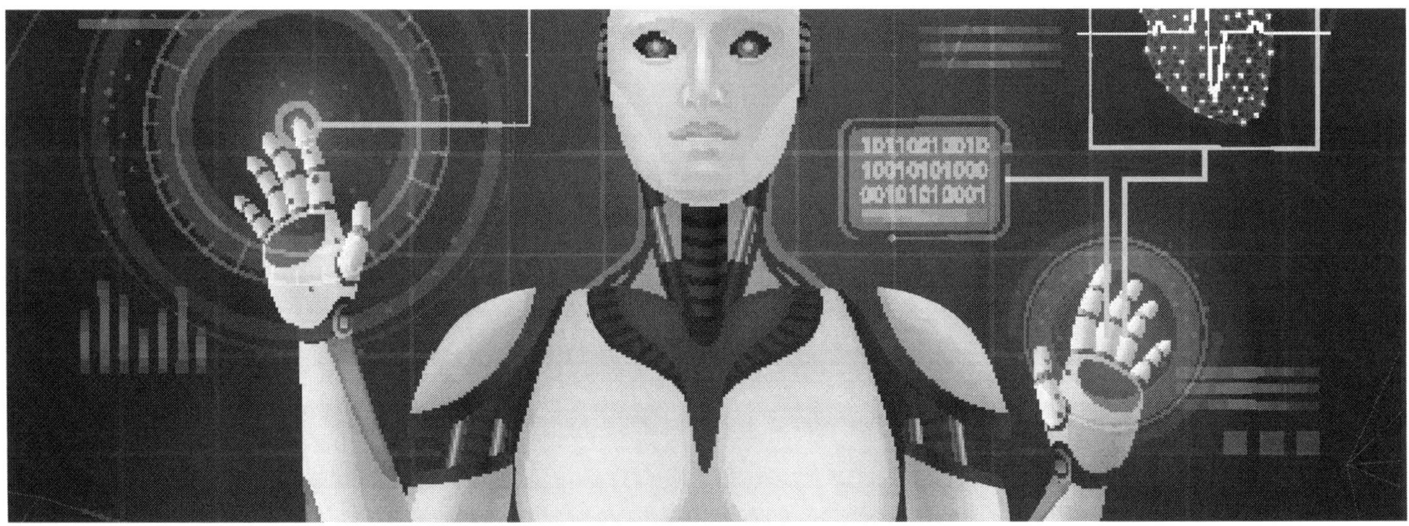

I don't write anything with a pen.

I believe that everyone has the right to be a little strange.

My hobby is to engrave all the inscriptions on the tablets to store information for centuries.

You may ask how I wrote this text back then, but they persuaded me to write a few sentences specifically for this book.

I like that I think over my every thought many times before I write. Once a year I make a plan for myself, I also write the main things that happened during the quarter in my life. I describe what is also happening in the world of important things.

Tablets are my way of self-expression and my favorite hobby. My meditation ritual.

Full autonomy of the 23rd century.

All parts of the planet (meaning every square kilometer) are officially inhabited (there are at least 100 people per square kilometer). It is the land that is considered here, difficult and high mountains, volcanoes and the like are not taken into account, as are seas with oceans, of course.

Full autonomy is the Internet anywhere in the world (underground and underwater too), electricity from solar panels, a borehole in every house, delivery of everything to anywhere in the world by drones (free of charge).

Now you can meet people everywhere, and it's good and bad. It is good because it has become a little freer, it is bad because the natural habitat of tens of thousands of animals has been violated.

However, every species of flora and fauna of the Earth was carefully removed to Greenspace and 95.7% took root and now live in new extraterrestrial lands.

We live in the center of the mountain range.

We moved to the center of the Mont Blanc mountain range in the western Alps. There are not so many places on the planet, and people have already begun to develop mountain ranges.

It may seem difficult at first, but with a universal vehicle that moves by air, sea and land, it is much easier. Drone delivery also works here. Around us, 30 hectares have been made warmer with the help of the Earth's climate control system (in orbit, using heat waves, they make a set temperature on certain parts of the earth).

In general, we like it, we don't feel as many people here as down, I don't want to talk about Switzerland, how many people there are now.

A royal family without a crown and a castle.

My name is George VII, I am the heir to the throne of the royal family from Great Britain.

However, I gave up my title and inheritance, instead I fell in love, got children, bought a few hectares of land, built a house. I live happily in the vicinity of Alicante, Spain.

I am the first naturally born girl in space.

When humanity decided to go to populate the new exoplanet Tharros, there was one big problem. To fly there for 1400 years, according to scientists, if you spend all the time in a special dream, then for a person it will be 140 years. We don't live that much yet, besides, young, healthy people who will begin active colonization should arrive on the planet.

That is why it was decided to "change" several generations during the flight. I am the beginning of the first such generation and my whole life is devoted to only one task - to be in a sleep until the age of 40, then to get pregnant from the chosen partner on the ship, to carry and raise a child with his father until his 18th birthday, along with training and understanding of his mission (he has the same as us). After that putting the child to sleep also until his 40 years (in fact, 220 years will pass for him). And for me to live the rest of my life on the ship, doing whatever my heart desires, I decided to write a few such lines.

I do not know how it could be otherwise, I just do not want to see my son in a long sleep, and I just look at him with my partner.

Revolution in space travel.

Now scientific excursions are being taken to my backyard on my ranch in Texas and a monument has been erected to the invention that changed space travel once and for all.

We are talking, of course, about everyone's favorite hypothermic stasis. I was able to improve it, refine it and make it safe in a shed in my backyard. I didn't really care where I was. The main thing is the opportunity to conduct experiments.

To be honest, I'm not particularly interested in space, people have already mastered more than one place in space and have become an interplanetary species, but I'm fine here, I've never been further than Texas, only 1 time in Washington.

I was more interested in the possibility of realizing the idea of long sleep and slowing down old age by 10 times. When an ordinary person passes 100 years and he dies, a person in hypothermic stasis passes 10 years and he can be returned to normal life and he will live. Yes, he slept for 100 years and still 10 years. This is also a problem, but he overcame 100 years in time and perhaps at this time progress is already different and due to new technologies he will live longer and better.

Time machine.

The time machine, how many times have we heard about it, hundreds if not thousands of attempts, but nothing ever worked out.

In 2056, on September 3, it turned out to move a person 1 minute ahead! The greatest discovery in the last 5 years. However, there is a significant drawback that they are still working on and do not know the answer.

Unfortunately, after passing through a time machine, a person overcomes 1 minute in one direction (let's call it the 4th axis of measurement), but the other directions (x, y, z, that is, its coordinates are accurate in the Universe) do not move, and since everything moves, including the planets and our Galaxy, the expansion of the Universe is 73.3 kilometers per second, which means that in 60 seconds (1 minute) a person moves away from the current point by 4398 kilometers. On all axes. We assumed anything for this, the first subject was in a spacesuit with an air reserve for 8 hours and he had uGPS (improved GPS on a Universal scale). We detected it in outer space by a sensor signal 4398 kilometers away and at the same moment flew after it. An hour later we were on Earth.

Movements have become possible but extremely dangerous at the moment. We need to understand how to overcome not only time but also coordinates in the universe in order to take into account the expansion of the Universe.

Eco-village.

We have 4 hectares of land in the southern part of Italy. This inheritance, worth at least 300 million dollars now, came to me from my great-grandfather, and he got it from his father.

Fertile lands, clean air, near the sea, own vineyard plantation and own wooden house. Isn't this paradise? We lived here with my wife and children for a long time, and one day we decided that it was time to invite guests to us. We built several wooden houses and began to rent them out. Later, a few years later, various festivals were already held here. I built and sold 8 more houses with my building company. An eco-village was formed here, which many people from all over the world wanted to come to.

Every year, at the harvest festival, we invite thousands of guests to celebrate and just have fun. It was quite warm outside, so we placed most of the guests in tents right in the middle of the vineyards.

Captain of a cruise ship.

I have been engaged in sewing curtains for 7 years, during this time I mastered this art and, it seems to me, succeeded quite well.

Our city stands by the river, which is connected to the sea after 120 kilometers, respectively, we have a port and quite a lot of different ships, from river to sea. Almost every evening after work, I went to the pier and looked at our widest river, at its peak it reached 3 kilometers wide. Therefore, sometimes it seemed that it was not a river, but a sea. I was often visited by thoughts about whether I should become a captain, surf the seas, and change my life radically.

But every time after such thoughts, I told myself "not today" and went home to rest.

One day everything changed, a tailwind blew to me in the form of an invitation to go on a sea adventure with my friend, where I will be a sailor. They had a task to deliver grain from our port in Italy to a port in South Africa. And there was a big shortage of sailors, one day I told my friend that I also wanted to swim and he invited me now.

It took more than 15 years before I became a full-fledged captain, I got a higher education, and my sister is now engaged in sewing curtains. I am already well over 50 and the sea gives me such vigor and energy that it cannot be compared with anything.

Inhabited exoplanets.

The planet Tharros turned out to be the most amazing and the farthest from our native Earth.

Let's start in order, when you step on the ground of Tharros, you have very dense grass under your feet, about 30 centimeters high, it is so thick and dense that if you fall on it from a few meters, you can't damage it, it will be like a mattress for you.

You see trees and do not understand how this is possible, basically they are all more than 1 kilometer high, up to about 1500 meters. A huge diameter of about 100 meters. It's like the most modern human skyscraper, only this tree. The leaves are the size of a person. It's scary, but it's also fascinating.

In the local ocean there are often waves of 100-150 meters (40-storey building), when on Earth the maximum is up to 19 meters (6-storey house).

Animals and plants are mostly 30% larger than ours. Local "tigers" can hold their breath underwater for up to 60 minutes and hunt there quietly. There are birds that hunt tigers, the size of these birds is like an ancient pterodactyl.

Basically, the places where a person settles resembles Switzerland of the 20th century, meadows of greenery, rivers, mountains, waterfalls. Animals are safe here and there will be no problems with our technologies, even if some bird wants to steal a person, it's simply impossible. Our artificial intelligence provides complete security and monitors everything and everywhere. In the case of something, the bird will not even have time to fly up to the person and it will be driven away.

Land plots are the most expensive asset.

Who would have thought in the 21st or 22nd century that land plots on Earth would become the most expensive asset that could only be on the planet.

The huge overpopulation of Earth has played its key role. Everyone wants to live comfortably and not be crowded in multi-storey buildings, for this everyone wants to have their own spacious 100-200 m2, that's how much in modern realities is considered the norm for a person. If it is 300-600 m2, then it is a rich person. Anything more than 1000 m2 is extremely rare, it is a super-rich person or the heir of huge lands earlier. There was a reform of the 22nd century where 90% of the land was seized from everyone for people who had nothing.

There are people who may own an entire island with an area of 50 thousand m2. There are several dozen such people in the world and these are the richest people on planet Earth.

That's why we have "spare", and now the main planets for life. Greenspace, Plaka and Tharros. Everyone can have 10,000 and 20,000 m2 there, for a decent life, as much as a person needs, and there will be so much.

The planet of savages.

Not far from the planet Tharros, another habitable planet was discovered, but many times smaller in size. The first colonists liked the planet and they called it Antistasi. However, the colonists were not simple, they were "rebels" who wanted a separate planet for themselves and did not want artificial intelligence at home. After all, there was no place in Australia anymore and from there all the rebels were sent to this separate planet.

As time went on, the Antistasi did not want to communicate with other planets, they lived their lives as "savages", so all the other planets thought, because only they refused artificial intelligence.

In the morning, at the end of February, long-range missiles flew at Tharros, Antistasi started the war. Of course, artificial intelligence repelled the missiles, but Antistasi did not want to give up and landed where there is no artificial intelligence and people, they began to go ahead on foot, but artificial intelligence stopped them anyway and sent them to their home. Antistasi became extremely unfriendly and stayed on their planet.

The first city on the ocean floor.

The Earth was and remains the most native place for any person anywhere in the universe. Only here there is overpopulation and, as a consequence, a shortage of land plots. A lot has been done to add land for people and now people have decided to take another step.

Build the first city on the ocean floor. Sources of eternal oxygen were found on one of the ocean sections, you can put a dome there, equipment to create the same climate as on Earth and there will be ideal conditions. Sunlight has long been learned to make artificially and its properties are 99.7% identical to the real one.

The construction took only 1 year and an additional 1,500 hectares appeared under the dome at a depth of more than 2 kilometers. Everyone could come to them in their universal car. There is nothing complicated here. All control has long been done by the machine independently and you only need to set the point to which you need to arrive / sail / arrive (this automatically adjusts everything and builds the most convenient and fastest route).

So people began to live underwater. Soon the city had to expand because there were a lot of people who wanted to buy plots of 300-400 m2.

One tablet = one day.

The latest invention of the 23rd century, one tablet = one day without food and water.

The tablet contains everything a person needs for proper nutrition, substances dissolve in the stomach during the day and saturate the body. At the same time, the pleasure of "saturation" is also present and it can be changed depending on the situation. Can be: light, medium and high saturation.

One tablet and you do whatever you want all day. At the same time, you can at least spend your whole life on such tablets and there will be no difference with normal nutrition.

We are all extremely different.

In the modern world, people have become so different that it is already difficult to even remember all possible subcultures, orientations, religions, hobbies and so on.

We have learned to live with each other against all odds, there are general rules, there is artificial intelligence and people. We all want to express our individuality and not hide what we are. In modern society this is the norm and there are no restrictions here anymore.

Exoplanet Pisti.

What people have dreamt of since the beginning of the exploration of outer space has happened - contact with intelligent life.

For more than 300 years, humanity has become an extraterrestrial species and settled on distant exoplanets suitable for life. All this became possible thanks to a multitude of inventions on Earth, literally hundreds of millions of people were involved in such a global and ambitious project as the colonization of another planet.

However, we still did not find intelligent life, although the flora and fauna were very similar to Earth's.

2612, the time when everything changed. On a normal Monday morning, ships unprecedented before began to land in the Neo city, they hovered as if without engines, resembled the shape of a flattened ball, were very streamlined, silver matte color, about the size of a football field and we counted 12 ships.

Everyone ran to the places where they landed, artificial intelligence and patrolmen were also there and were already preparing for defense if anything (we still had weapons but underground, but only artificial intelligence had access and in this case he could use it).

A part of the ship "disappeared", it resembled our doors, only this part disappeared somewhere. The creatures that were on the ship appeared in it. They look somewhat similar to people, also arms and legs, only more elastic, and it feels like they have fewer bones, while the skin color is similar to ours, the head is about 5% larger than ours, they are dressed in the same clothes from a material unknown to me before.

They came down, we looked at each other, they looked at us and seemed to be saying something, but we didn't understand, then they looked at each other and it seemed that they had a dialog with each other, although no one heard anything. Their mouth was very small and they did not open it once, their nose was also small and flattened. Artificial intelligence realized that they communicate using telepathy. He turned himself to all possible "channels" and began to send signals in the form of pictures of himself (the patrolman). After a second, all the aliens looked at him and approached him, they sent him a "signal" with the decoding of their language, where all the basics were contained and tied to certain pictures, places and events so that any intelligent being could decipher. Artificial intelligence processed the information for 10 seconds and then was able to understand the whole essence of their way of communication, language and all the nuances. After that, he became our translator.

The moment they understood each other, the aliens suddenly decided to leave us. We will leave our coordinates with an invitation to artificial intelligence.

The first contact of mankind with another intelligent life took place. The moment that everyone has been waiting for for more than 3 thousand years.

The first "soaring" city in the sky.

After the development of marine spaces and in particular the entire ocean, humanity on Earth realized that there is still air. Making a soaring city turned out to be not a very difficult task with modern technologies and artificial intelligence calculations. After 7 months of construction, the city was ready and the first people settled on their land plots on the soaring city above the oceans. At the same time, the city stood statically and only occasionally aligned its location.

My life has changed.

Doing your own thing has become so popular that almost all my friends have made their own family business. I did not dare in any way because the work at the local university was not bad. At one point, the idea came to me that in my business I would be able to realize all my desires, the author's methodology and teach students broader knowledge than the standard program. So I finally decided and opened my own private office for the professional improvement of students' practical skills. After some time, I was able to fully complete my author's methodology and began teaching it to my groups of students. The result was colossal, my students won all the Olympiads and were the best. Such a technique would not be allowed in an ordinary university, but since this is my business, I can try everything, somewhere I will lose, and somewhere I will win so much that I will understand that this is the meaning of my business, independence and my way, with my defeats and victories.

Milky Way. *My last message.*

We became an interplanetary species, made teleports and a time machine, were able to defeat all diseases known to people, increased the average life expectancy to 154 years, and artificial intelligence became our state.

I think even in the wildest expectations of the 21st or 22nd century, people could not imagine what awaits our descendants in some 200-400 years. Often people don't think about it because they themselves won't be there anymore, such thinking is wrong. Modern humans, of the 27th century, think as a whole. To make humanity an interplanetary species costs the lives of thousands of people, hundreds of millions of hours of labor. Now, as a species, we have gone far beyond the original limits of our "destiny". According to forecasts of artificial intelligence, the planet Earth has about 5 million years left to "live". This is a lot, but within the frames of the Universe it is nothing. Our species could have disappeared faster than the dinosaurs disappeared (they lived about 250 million years as a species, humanity now lives about 3 million years as a species). However, we have "insured" ourselves and are looking for new planets and exploring them.

There is one small but. All of humanity is in the same Milky Way galaxy. Yes, yes, my reader, you have understood correctly. Humanity decided to leave the Galaxy and explore others. There is only one more small but. The distance to the first habitable planet outside our galaxy is 23,651,826,175,000,000 kilometers. Our advanced ships can fly at 0.5 of the speed of light. To get there, it will take 50,000 years to be in flight. Such colossal distances exist only in space. 50 thousand years of being in flight. We have already been in flight for 1400 years during the exploration of the planet Tharros far from Earth, several generations changed there in space before getting there and starting colonization.

This time, humanity will have to make 157 generations (if you give birth at 50). How possible is this project, whether people will be able to bring it to the end. Is this project worth the insane colossal investments from each of the planets? Dozens of questions, not so many answers.

One thing we know for sure, we have to do it. The flight is 50 thousand years long, guess what generation I am and what I am doing now. I think you guessed it, I am the first generation. With my partner we have already raised our three children and now we have to spend about 50 more years on the ship before our death, no longer in a sleep, but in life. I'm sitting on the front of the ship, there is a large panoramic window in front of a special nanomaterial that cannot be penetrated by space debris. I opened a can of beer, I looked into the distance, the realization that I left everything on my planet and went on this crazy mission scares me sometimes. I am already about 70 years old, we have brought up our children and put them to sleep until their 50th anniversary when they will repeat our fate, and we are flying. I got on board and we went when I was 20 years old.

The majestic emptiness of the Milky Way. That's what I call the space around me. I laugh at humanity, what kind of "parasites" we are in a good way. We will settle in the most remote and inaccessible places, we will settle everywhere and you will not drive us out later.

This is my last message, there are still 49 thousand 680 years left to fly. It's scary to even imagine. About as long as our species exists in its intelligent form of life. Now there is so much more to fly forward until we leave our Milky Way Galaxy.

The majestic and endless emptiness of the Milky Way.

Printed in Great Britain
by Amazon